Praise

'*Help Wanted* is a breath of fresh air in a world of stale HR doctrine. It refuses to treat people as data points or hospitality as performance. Instead, it reclaims the soul of service – the spark that turns ordinary encounters into unforgettable experiences. In these pages, you'll find a brave, human-centric alternative to traditional hiring: one that celebrates curiosity, kindness, and courage as competitive advantages. Nicole doesn't just challenge the status quo; she offers a practical, poetic roadmap for building teams that thrive. A people-centric future of hospitality is surely what we all crave at a soul level. Read it not as a manual, but as a manifesto for hiring human magic.'
— **David Carruthers**, hospitality strategist and mentor, and founder, Future of Hospitality

'*Help Wanted* is the guidebook maverick leaders have been waiting for. It's packed with practical tools to help you hire for human magic. At Hospitality Mavericks, we believe the best leaders know that people are their greatest advantage – and work hard to hire, nurture, and lead them with heart and kindness. If you want to build a profitable business as a force for good and dare to be different, this book is for you – because mavericks hire for impact: people, community, and the planet.'
— **Michael Tingsager**, host and creator of the *Hospitality Mavericks* podcast and Head of Customer Experience, noon

'In *Help Wanted*, Nicole taps into a powerful idea – one with the potential to transform the hospitality industry from the inside. She reminds us that the magic we strive to create for our guests begins long before they arrive. It starts with how we recruit. To deliver unforgettable guest experiences, we must make our hiring process just as thoughtful, personal, and human. That means taking the time to handpick those rare individuals who naturally bring warmth, authenticity, and a genuine human connection to every interaction.'
— **Larry Korman**, CEO, hotel aka + aka hotel residences

'*Help Wanted* is the book our industry has been waiting for. It redefines hospitality from the inside out – reminding us that true luxury begins with how we hire, nurture, and honour people. This is HR with heart, courage, and soul.'
— **Paulo de Tarso**, restaurateur and founder, Paulo de Tarso Hospitality

'Every hospitality leader needs to read *Help Wanted* because doing the same thing over and over and expecting different results is, as they say, the definition of insanity. Nicole has always been an HR rebel, and in her exciting new book, she shows from experience how we can all break free from tired recruitment norms and create our own human magic. This is true "hearts and minds" material – a guide to making the difference we all strive to achieve for our people, culture, and businesses.'
— **Lizzie Bullen**, Group People and Culture Director, Iconic Luxury Hotels

'This book is a genuine standout. It makes you think differently, see possibilities where others see barriers, and reminds you what authentic leadership looks like. Nicole's insights are fresh, practical, and full of heart, capturing the same energy and vision she brings to any room. Every travel and hospitality leader will find a new perspective and renewed purpose in these pages. *Help Wanted* is an instant addition to my "Lucy Library" – the books that inspire me to lead with more humanity and courage. Read it, share it, and let it challenge you to lead with heart.'
— **Lucy Wedderburn**, Group Head of People, Virgin Limited Edition

'I couldn't put this book down! Every HR and hospitality leader needs a copy of *Help Wanted*. It brings us back to genuine human care and connection. Filled with real stories that remind us of the impact of feelings, not just with guests, but within our teams, this book re-centres what hospitality hiring should be. Nicole shares her years of maverick experience – as she famously often says, "Lift others as you climb." *Help Wanted* has lifted and inspired me to new heights – a true nugget of a book.'
— **Peter Avis FIH**, Business Development and Community Engagement Manager, London Hilton on Park Lane

'This book is an absolute gem. Nicole's perspective perfectly captures the importance of hiring the right people to create a successful hotel, showing how

personality is as essential as skill and experience in crafting a bespoke guest experience. Her insights reveal how to build your dream team. *Help Wanted* is a must-read for anyone who wants to level up their hospitality and create unforgettable experiences through their people.'
   — **Hannah Davies**, Managing Director,
      GH Executive

'The idea that hiring is an act of human alchemy is pure genius. *Help Wanted* puts human magic at the centre of how we find and grow teams – a true compass for the people space and a "before-and-after" read for leaders everywhere. As we embrace innovation, it reminds us of what truly makes businesses and humans thrive.'
   — **Simona Barbieri**, founder and CEO,
      HubDot

Help Wanted

The **rule-breaking guide** to hiring an extraordinary team of hospitality alchemists

Nicole Antonio-Gadsdon

R^ethink

First published in Great Britain in 2025
by Rethink Press (www.rethinkpress.com)

© Copyright Nicole Antonio-Gadsdon

All rights reserved. No part of this publication may be reproduced, stored in, or introduced into a retrieval system, or transmitted, in any form, or by any means (electronic, mechanical, photocopying, recording, or otherwise) without the prior written permission of the publisher.

The right of Nicole Antonio-Gadsdon to be identified as the author of this work has been asserted by her in accordance with the Copyright, Designs and Patents Act 1988.

This book is sold subject to the condition that it shall not, by way of trade or otherwise, be lent, resold, hired out, or otherwise circulated without the publisher's prior consent in any form of binding or cover other than that in which it is published and without a similar condition including this condition being imposed on the subsequent purchaser.

Help comment icon by Setyo Ari Wibowo | the Noun Project

Back cover and p275 photography by Gemma Hazelwood Photography | @gemmahazelwoodphotography

*For Chris and Lily – my two heartbeats
and reminders of what matters*

Contents

Preface	1
Introduction	5
PART ONE The Why	15
1 Turbulence Warning	17
2 Human Connection: The Hidden Pulse Of Your Competitive Advantage	33
3 Overview Of The Unorthodox Interviewer's Guide	49
PART TWO The What	63
4 Spec'd To Fail: What You Lose When You Hire By The Book	65
5 The Anatomy Of A Hospitality Alchemist	77

6	Alchemy By Numbers: The Skills You Can't Train But Must Find	85
7	Interview Mise En Place: Prepare To Welcome Your Candidate	95
8	The Golden Rules Of Unorthodox Interviewing	105
9	How To Host Interviews Like A Hearty Supper Club Gathering	115

PART THREE	The How	123
10	Appetiser – Starting With Amuse-Bouche Questions	125
11	Entrée: Revealing Your Candidate's Super Skills Combo	133
12	Dessert – Wrapping Up With Intention	141

PART FOUR	The Super Skills	151
13	Super Skill 1: Empathy	153
14	Super Skill 2: Kindness	163
15	Super Skill 3: Curiosity	171
16	Super Skill 4: Creativity	181

17	Super Skill 5: Unlearn Learning	189
18	Super Skill 6: Gratitude	197
19	Super Skill 7: Vulnerability	207
20	Super Skill 8: Courage	217
21	Super Skill 9: Resilience	225
22	Super Skill 10: Purpose Connection	235

Conclusion: If Not Now, When?	243
Bibliography	249
Further Resources	261
Glossary	267
Acknowledgements	271
The Author	275

Preface

This is not your average HR manual, and I am not your average HR practitioner. I'm therefore going to start this book with a brief explanation of why I – an HR rebel – have written this book, with the aim of transforming hospitality hiring from predictable humdrum to human magic.

As an HR innovator for luxury boutique hotels, I often work in paradise locations with jaw-dropping natural beauty and picture-perfect properties. A dark shadow lingers, though – the uncomfortable connection between service and sacrifice – tired hiring rituals sorting people by stereotypes and stuffing human potential into rigid roles. Too many candidates end up being shoehorned into roles based on outdated hierarchies and assumptions about culture, class, and competence. Token tweaks to old recruitment systems and traditional thinking no longer satisfy the realities of today's guest expectations, employee ambitions, and business needs.

This book was born from frustration and fierce hope. I have spent over twenty years working with pioneering hoteliers and hospitality leaders who dare to create cultures and signature experiences centred on soul, not just service. Sadly, too often their recruitment strategies and hiring processes – soulless, stiff, and stuck in outdated scripts – lagged behind their innovations.

I began writing this book in October 2021, but the origin story goes further back. In 2015 I launched my first blog, *The HR Rabbit Hole*, a rebellious outpost where I experimented with creative HR concepts and rule-breaking prototypes. It was my sandbox – my personal dare to do things differently and my first public step away from the conventional HR path. That blog became my test kitchen, where I deconstructed tired HR formulas and recreated them with flavour, heart, and timeless human truths. Over the years this evolved into my consulting agency, Banana Pepper HR, where my belief in the transformative potential of unorthodox hiring was distilled into a collection of cultural brand-builder recipes and a wider body of work in ALT-HR – a bold, inventive alternative to conventional HR practices, designed with hospitality in mind.

PREFACE

Time and again I saw how traditional hiring approaches failed to uncover the vital human qualities that breathe life into brand promises and make hospitality magic.

I stopped sticking to the interview script and listened for stories. I asked unexpected questions. In every unforgettable hire and remarkable team assembled, I discovered the same pattern: a constellation of Super Skills hiding in plain sight, waiting to be welcomed to the table. These were not soft skills, often quoted and undervalued. They were super (human) powers, and they deserved a new framework.

Those first revelations have now evolved into the unorthodox interviewer's guide to hiring human magic you now hold in your hands. Here you will find more than just a critique of hiring. You will discover a bold alternative:

- Practical, poetic tools to help you identify the people who can bring hospitality to life
- A Three-Course Conversation interview framework
- Ten essential Super Skills

This book doesn't ask you to toss everything out. It invites you to reimagine your hiring not as a process to endure but as a hospitality experience to elevate people, brand, and culture, and create shared stories that build brands of uncommon distinction.

I hope this book becomes your well-thumbed companion – not just another theory-filled business book, but a practical rebellion guide you can apply straightaway in your business. I wrote this book because hospitality, at its best, reaffirms our shared humanity and is nothing short of magic.

Together, let's rewrite the rules, reimagine the interview, and hire for human magic.

Your seat at the table is already reserved.

Introduction

Our world is no longer simply volatile, uncertain, complex, and ambiguous (VUCA). It is volcanic, and a volcanic world demands a new hiring playbook. Sticking to outdated rules – such as traditional industrial-era management methods or relying on the same strategies that once led to your business's success – will not work today.

Cosmetic changes to years-entrenched practices no longer work in today's business realities, nor do they meet guest expectations or satisfy employee ambitions. The hospitality industry's moment of truth has arrived, and it is as exacting in its demands as a special-attention guest staying at a luxury hotel. The decisions and actions you make now will determine whether you fail or achieve sustainable success in the future.

Do not let this opportunity to pivot slip through your fingers.

You know that hospitality, done right, is the highest expression of our humanity. This time-honoured art elevates both guests and team members through meaningful, memorable experiences.

Imagine you have made changes to your operations, upgraded your technology, reconfigured your service offering, and renegotiated terms with your suppliers. What is next? Now is the time to reimagine your recruitment and hiring processes to match all those other improvements.

Let us assume you are a visionary who thinks differently. You know that putting people at the heart of your business is vital for survival and success. You are determined to cultivate an environment brimming with authenticity, where human connections flourish, and team members succeed as unique contributors, not interchangeable assets.

A radical movement quietly brewing

Most HR and business books are relics of an industrial era, discounting the nuanced complexities of today's world of work and the human magic that fuels extraordinary businesses. Even those that recognise human magic rarely explain how to attract, hire, and, retain it.

INTRODUCTION

This guide isn't a cure-all for your hiring troubles, but it provides a solid starting point. It encourages you to interview differently, break free from cookie-cutter competency constraints, and escape the vicious cycle of hiring more of the same as everyone else.

If you feel this is like the stirrings of a radical underground HR movement, you are right. I am inviting you to join the rebellion against outdated recruitment rules that serve collapsing traditional business structures and fail to keep pace with rapid social shifts.

This is about more than efficiently filling roles and hitting your vacancy closure target. It is the pursuit of discovering human magic. This unseen yet unmistakable presence breathes vitality into your culture, infusing every guest experience and team interaction with a life-affirming human connection and brand distinction.

The standard operating procedure (SOP) for HR hiring does not provide the necessary guidance. What you need is an unconventional interviewing framework and hiring system.

Have you ever found yourself looking at a candidate and then reviewing their CV, feeling that something just does not add up? They aced the interview. Their qualifications, knowledge, and experience meet all the criteria. Your intuition keeps whispering, though, that you are missing something crucial – insights that might not be reflected in your standard scorecards or typical interview questions. That nagging feeling persists because the 'something' vital for making the right hiring decision remains hidden in a space where tangible technical skills end and human qualities begin.

The unfortunate reality is that all too often, polished résumés and textbook responses mask toxic attitudes, and values mismatch. Traditional interview questions discourage candidates from showcasing their vibrant individuality and genuine character, which are precisely the qualities needed to assemble an extraordinary hospitality team. Not long ago, technical skills were considered the prized golden ticket for a perfect hire, while soft skills were dismissed as weak or nice-to-haves. That is no longer the case. Today soft skills serve as strong indicators of standout brands that survive and thrive in this rapidly changing landscape.

Drawing inspiration from trailblazing minds in the culinary arts, marketing, science, philosophy, and entrepreneurship, I recognised patterns and alternatives that traditional HR often overlooks. The more I explored, the clearer it became that hiring could be magical, a process of alchemy and a source of competitive edge in a crowded market.

The initial prototype interview framework was quietly developed for personal use. Over time, I refined it, observing where it worked and where it did not. I adapted and shared it with clients to help ease persistent hiring headaches. This conversational approach did more than humanise interviews; it provided exceptional clarity, stripping away façades to reveal the remarkable individuals behind the mask. Beneath social constructs and surface differences such as class, nationality, and gender, a universal set of 'superhuman skills' – which I call Super Skills – quietly bubbled, waiting to be discovered and brought to centre stage.

This is not just another hiring manual. It is a mindset shift, a field guide, and a call to arms. In each chapter you will find unconventional frameworks, practical techniques, real-world examples, and a dose of daring.

You will learn how to:

- Rethink how you define 'talent'
- Ask better, deeper, more human questions
- Hire individuals who light up a room and elevate the whole team
- Cultivate a distinctive culture that thrives on connection, not compliance

This unorthodox hiring guide invites you to reframe the interview conversation and move from transactional hiring to transformational connection. It presents a rogues gallery of bad hire character types that pose dangers to your operation, along with tips on how to identify and steer clear of them. It shows you how to assemble a team of hospitality alchemists, and what to ask in an interview to reveal their true magic.

This book is written for the rebels, the rule breakers, the reinventors, and especially for the human-first visionaries who believe that hospitality starts in-house.

In your hands is a guide built for action:

- **Part One: The Why.** This first part gives the context of hiring for human magic and explains why it matters now more than ever.

- **Part Two: The What.** Here you'll find the unorthodox new approach to interviews, designed to reveal candidates' Super Skills.

- **Part Three: The How.** These chapters will reveal the delights of the Three-Course Conversation interview framework – a whole new approach to uncovering candidates' strengths.

- **Part Four: The Super Skills.** This final part explains in depth the Super Skills, which you'll find listed below. Each chapter provides ready-to-use, connection-rich interview questions to get you started.

Use this guide as a conversation starter, internal training prompt, or personal development tool when rewriting your recruitment strategy to boost your hospitality brand. Keep it visible. Use it. Add your own

Super Skills questions to it. And practise unorthodox interviewing. If in doubt, trust and be guided by your human magic.

The ten Super Skills of human magic

Every luxury boutique hotel, restaurant, and private island hospitality business I partnered with became a living canvas to refine my hypothesis. Real human stories uncovered during conversational interviews revealed evidence and profound insights into exceptional skills and human qualities. These are condensed in Part Four into the ten essential Super Skills, which create meaningful human connections in genuine hospitality:

1. **Empathy** – intuitively sensing and responding meaningfully to others

2. **Kindness** – radiating genuine warmth and thoughtful care

3. **Curiosity** – enjoying an exploratory, questioning mindset

4. **Creativity** – improvising and solving problems imaginatively

5. **Unlearn learning** – letting go of the obsolete and embracing the new

6. **Gratitude** – expressing appreciation with meaning and generosity

7. **Vulnerability** – being open and authentic

8. **Courage** – boldly acting beyond conventional thinking and the status quo

9. **Resilience** – maintaining grace under pressure, with the ability to bounce back and bounce forwards

10. **Purpose connection** – aligning personal values and motivation with the organisation's vision and mission

Imagine hotel lobbies where laughter bubbles freely from behind the front desk. Kitchens that purr with creative joy, dignity, and pride. Imagine entire teams collaborating like jazz ensembles in full swing, improvising, trusting, and thriving, creating extraordinary, customised guest experiences.

If you are looking for a plug-and-play hiring template, stop reading now. However, if you are weary of tinkering with the ill-suited, outdated competency-based interview questions that no longer meet your business's urgent need to hire only the right people to bring your unique hospitality brand to life, keep reading.

This book is the unorthodox interviewer's guide we have needed but never managed to find, until now. I have poured my heart and soul into creating exactly what is needed to defy convention and assemble a team that will help you build a human-led hospitality business against all odds.

INTRODUCTION

These are your unconventional field notes for uncovering the rare, and often overlooked, brilliance needed to assemble your extraordinary team. It is designed to help you hire individuals who are not just technically proficient but also virtuosos at creating remarkable guest experiences. It shows you how to find, interview for, and hire human magic – the secret formula that distinguishes your business and significantly impacts long-term profitability.

With this book I am taking a strategic bet on you. I am betting on human magic, our shared humanity, as an unquestionable strategic edge. Your competitors may hesitate. Will you step up and bet on it, too?

Your action decides what happens next.

Ready to challenge convention, unlock the magic within each candidate's story, and free your team's exponential potential?

Let's crack on.

PART ONE
THE WHY

1
Turbulence Warning

Buckle up. Our world is tilting on its axis, hurtling us into an era of constant, relentless change. We are navigating a category-five storm of rapid evolution, and the turbulence is real. Chaos echoes across every area of our lives, resulting from COVID-19, conflict, climate upheaval, societal shifts, and rising living costs. These are not distant headlines; they are daily jolts forcing us to re-examine everything we once believed to be steadfast.

The human connection crisis

Despite advances in technology that bring us hyper-connectivity, we are facing a profound crisis of human *disconnection*. Gallup's 2025 report *State of the Global Workplace* (Gallup, 2025) states that global employee engagement has fallen from 23% to 21%, with 62% disengaged and 17% actively disengaged. Manager engagement fell from 30% to 27%, and when managers disengage, so do their teams. As team engagement erodes, customer relationships, cohesion, and productivity follow.

Talent Strategy for Growth: A CHRO's guide (Gartner, 2025) warns that while growth remains a priority for CEOs, people issues now top the list of business risks, outpacing cost management, operations, and market competition. The CIPD's report 'Benchmarking Employee Turnover' (CIPD, 2024) reveals that hospitality in the UK has the highest staff turnover at 52%, driving soaring recruitment and training costs.

In 2023, supported by the Institute of Hospitality, eHotelier published a white paper titled *The Industry's Future Skills Needs* (eHotelier, 2023), identifying the current skills gaps and the most in-demand skills for hospitality to meet the immediate and future needs of a changing industry. Businesses were facing chronic staff shortages and declining customer confidence, and they were increasingly questioning the existing business models. While the importance of operational and professional skills such as problem solving, communication, and cooperation with others remain, eHotelier reported that the most sought-after skills and personality traits to recruit and promote are:

- Creativity and innovation
- Empathy and cultural awareness
- Passion
- Ethical values such as trust, honesty, and integrity

We are facing a human crisis in businesses and workplaces that demands more than cosmetic tweaks to broken systems.

How did we end up here?

Disasters rarely arrive with fanfare. As Ernest Hemingway wrote, in an exchange between two characters in *The Sun Also Rises* (Hemingway, 1926):

'How did you go bankrupt?'
'Two ways. Gradually, then suddenly.'

The gradual onset of disaster is true of business leaders ignoring the shifting ground beneath their feet. In the face of change, they often cling to familiar handrails: traditional hiring practices, comfortable mindsets, and policies designed for stability rather than adaptability.

Standing still is perilous. Complacency manifests as outdated systems quietly compounding poor decisions into bad outcomes. Hiring as you have always done, relying on generic job descriptions and outdated competency models, breeds mediocrity and stifles innovation.

As Dr Vikki Barnes reminds us in *Free Happiness* (Barnes, 2021), radical acceptance starts with:

- Facing reality head-on
- Acknowledging hardship experiences and deciding not to be consumed by them
- Choosing hope and optimism
- Taking clear, constructive action

That action begins in designing your culture for new realities and building teams that are wired for agility, adaptability, and creativity.

The storm is not passing; the forecast is for squalls in the foreseeable future. Now is the time to pivot – the clock is ticking to turn crisis into opportunity.

Crisis is not the enemy – inaction is

Waiting for luck is not a strategy; inaction poses a greater risk. The question is not how long the turbulence will last. It is whether you will collapse under it or ride it out on top.

Amid the chaos, opportunity glimmers. While cold business data and sympathetic internal systems provide stability, they are not the source of fresh opportunities and the way forward. Finding a new way in an unpredictable environment relies on fluid brilliance, brave action, and authentic human connection.

Maverick leaders are emerging. They reject cookie-cutter cultures, pursue human-led hospitality, and celebrate individuality as a revolutionary stance.

The AI paradox: The virtual Hotel California

Artificial intelligence offers dazzling efficiency but also serious risks. As algorithms handle repetitive tasks and carry out transactions, our unique human qualities (think empathy, curiosity, creativity, vulnerability) are in danger of becoming dulled or, worse, diminished.

On the one hand, we risk becoming trapped in a sterile digital Hotel California – a dazzling and seductive yet soulless environment – checked in and unable to escape. On the other hand, when steered wisely, AI can liberate us from the mundane, enabling us to concentrate more on emotional nuance and context, care that matters, and creating meaningful connections. Technology must serve humanity, not replace it.

Senthil Ayyappan's article for *MarketingProfs* (Ayyappan, 2025) states that we must amplify authenticity and prioritise human connection. He writes that 'Authenticity, in many ways, means to be *human*. […] we need humans behind the work to drive this somewhat illusive feeling of relatable real-ness.'

Making the illusive tangible requires the human touch, and employees behind it with unique skills. Ayyappan shares four skills to focus on: experimentation, customer interaction, storytelling, and collaboration.

In this unpredictable age, competitive advantage and long-term survival belong to businesses that augment irreplaceable human attributes, not to those who outsource their culture and automate their humanity.

What is (and isn't) genuine hospitality

As part of my research for this book, I gathered case studies and stories. This was a fantastic opportunity to reconnect with former colleagues and clients through questions (mine), responses (theirs), and conversations (ours). One such interaction was with Lisa Redfern, a past guest services manager at Necker Island and former training lead in the people team for Virgin Limited Edition properties in the British Virgin Islands. As the co-founder and lead interventionist of The Barefoot Trainer BVI, she now partners with luxury resort managers and private island owners to transform their guest service teams into super-connectors and epic hosts.

The question that sparked one standout conversation was, *What is genuine hospitality?*

Lisa shared two stories from her own experience in guest services operations, changing the names to protect the guests' privacy.

Story 1

The guest services team orchestrated a surprise wedding proposal on a private island in the Eastern Caribbean. Picture this: A skydiver nails his landing close to a woman casually strolling on a pristine white-sand beach. He approaches, drops to one knee, pulls out the ring, and proposes. She screams '*Yes!*', then the champagne flows.

The James Bond-style drama and flawless execution of this scene created an unforgettable experience for the couple.

Story 2

Mr Smith's life changed during a secluded island retreat. Previously paralysed in a climbing accident, he watched from the sidelines as his family enjoyed the beach activities.

Moved by his situation, the hospitality team got to work. Maintenance created a safe way to carry Mr Smith down the steep, rocky steps to the small, private beach. Guest services arranged a picnic in a shaded spot. With Mrs Smith's encouragement, two members of the watersports team helped Mr Smith into the calm water, where he used specially customised floats to swim alongside his family for the first time since his accident. There was not a dry eye among the family or the team as they shared a precious moment of normalcy.

Which of these two stories do you find best represents genuine hospitality, and why?

The first story is a clear example of a flawlessly executed guest experience, filled with frills and bursting with wow factors. Although the task is finished, it feels incomplete. There is no mirror effect, nor an emotional connection between the guests and the hospitality team. Where is the magic?

The second story tells a different tale. It fills the gap with the essential, missing element: human magic. The experience feels more complete and fulfilling. It strikes an emotional chord, creating ripples of warmth, joy, and genuine empathy. A challenge is transformed into a cherished experience, a moment of shared joy, and meaningful human connection. It touches both the team and the guests as well as us as readers. Ultimately, it reaffirms our shared humanity.

These two stories show that genuine Hospitality (with a capital H) differs from mere service:

Story 1	Story 2
Process-focused	People-focused
Transactional	Emotional
Service-driven	Experience-led
Thought	Felt
Business as usual	Business unusual

Authentic hospitality is a skilful blend of technical expertise and intuitive understanding. Ultimately, the most important and often elusive factor is human connection. You might not be able to pinpoint its subtle rhythm; however, when you experience it, you recognise it instantly. More importantly, you feel it as well.

Hiring for genuine hospitality follows a similar pattern. It involves hand-selecting remarkable individuals with flair – true artisans of hospitality who embody these qualities perfectly. I call this *human magic*.

Cookie-cutter service: The silent assassin

Rigid service standards cannot create the one-of-a-kind experiences guests crave. When standard scripts replace conversations, the service becomes robotic. Smug, efficient perfection repels more than it attracts. Zombie teams (aka the working dead) drain life force and energy from your operation.

Today's guests demand more than functional transactions. They crave heart-crafted, frictionless, human-led experiences delivered with warmth, adaptability, and individuality. As Gregor Nassief, owner of Secret Bay, puts it: 'Hospitality is really about caring for others – being part of people's lives in a meaningful, transformative and lasting way' (Britell, 2022).

This happens when team members break free from the constraints of box-ticking, cold, efficient service delivery. The team then become welcoming hosts, creating spaces where people feel they belong. Impresarios in the art of hospitality, crafting authentic experiences one by one, according to the needs and wishes of each guest. A united unordinary team contributing immeasurable value to your business.

The unseen force behind magical guest experiences

Marketing icon Seth Godin predicted that sustainable success would belong to businesses built on authentic connection, not mechanical efficiency (Godin, 2014). Bernadette Jiwa echoes this in *Story Driven* (Jiwa, 2018): 'We're moving towards the formulation of a new value equation – one that rewards work that is carried out with heart and rewards businesses that are driven by purpose before profits.'

Pioneers like Zingerman's Community of Businesses have built successful companies by making people – employees, customers, and suppliers – the core of their strategy. Over the past four decades, Zingerman's has grown from a single deli into ten businesses, employing over 750 people and generating more than $70 million in annual revenue, all while staying true to its purpose and values (Zingerman's, no date).

Focusing on what is most meaningful and uplifting is vital, as Danny Meyer summarises (Meyer, 2006): 'In the end, what's most meaningful is creating positive, uplifting outcomes for human experiences and human relationships. Business, like life, is all about how you make people feel. It's that simple, and it's that hard.'

It's simple, yes; but it is not common practice.

Your difference is your superpower

What if your ultimate competitive advantage was not being better, but being unmistakably different?

As Srini Rao writes in *Unmistakable* (Rao, 2016), you shouldn't chase being the best; you should become the only one.

Simone Biles is not just the best gymnast in the world; she exists in a league of her own, with her only competition being herself. You want your business to stand in similar territory, being distinctive, peerless, and impossible to copy. Be like Biles – allow your commitment to your craft, values, and difference to create a transformative impact beyond your niche discipline.

As Bernadette Jiwa writes in *Difference* (Jiwa, 2014): 'Creating difference isn't about beating competition. It's about closing the gap between what exists and what could be.' It takes courage to stand apart from common practice and embrace new discoveries. The scientific establishment took over eighty years to officially recognise umami as the fifth basic taste – along with the familiar sweet, sour, salty, and bitter (Umami Information Center, no date). Like Marmite, your distinct flavour will divide opinion, and that is the point. You will not be everyone's cup of tea, but you will matter deeply to those who truly count.

In our fast-paced world, you might be fortunate to have five years before your competitors start to close in. Do not settle for filling rooms or turning tables. Hone your human edge while you can. Craft experiences that hook your guests and compel them to return. You want to leave them smitten with your signature brand of hospitality.

Will you flourish or flounder?

Today's winners are those who bet on inimitable human qualities, which are the source of the undeniable magic of our shared humanity. Physical features such as location, interior design, menus, and amenities are easily imitated. However, soul, story, and signature guest experiences built on authentic human connection? That is unhackable.

Invest in people – 'idiosyncratic miracle workers', as Seth Godin calls them (Godin, 2014). In Hospitality's harsh reality, trends fade fast and gimmicks age quickly. Betting on universal human principles never goes out of style. Hire your team of boundary pushers who live to create magic, and then keep raising the bar.

In these times of rapid change, if your hiring strategy still relies on rigid recruiting rules and stale selection processes, you are jeopardising your business's future. David Chang, founder of Momofuku, says it plainly: 'If you're still using what worked for you in the past, you are screwed' (Chang, 2019).

Determined to break free from the constraints of the conventional interview format, I deliberately deviated from standard scripts and engaged in what many dismissed as small talk. Remarkably, these informal exchanges uncovered twenty-four-carat golden nuggets: authentic humans brimming with personality, dreams, values, life lessons, and those all-important Super Skills. The real person behind the interview performance began to appear unfiltered.

These discoveries consistently led to more informed and better hiring decisions, ultimately resulting in a stronger alignment between candidates' values and the company culture. As Bernadette Jiwa writes in her book *Meaningful* (Jiwa, 2015), 'data analytics can't always measure what matters most'.

I did not rush to crunch recruitment and retention ROI metrics. While they are important, they are never a priority for me. I was far more curious about something deeper and seemingly out of reach: how to create conditions where the qualities for authentic human connection and genuine character consistently emerge during the interview. Inspired by Bernadette, I wondered: What if I could create a structured interview framework that encouraged prized human qualities to emerge consistently and be evaluated?

Hospitality has always been at the forefront of innovation in food, interior design, architecture, and guest experiences, but its HR practices often remain frozen in time. That changes now with this book.

Abandon homogeneous hiring. Reject standard interviews that yield standard results. Assemble your team of remarkable human connectors – a band of hospitality alchemists capable of creating guest experiences that energise your brand.

Empathy. Kindness. Curiosity. Creativity. These are just four of the Super Skills needed to brew your brand's signature feel.

You may be curious about how to find this elusive human magic, and you are in the right place. I wrote this guide to show you exactly how to hire human magic for your business. Take a deep breath, and let's dive into the deep.

> **REFLECTION PROMPTS**
> - Is your hiring process uncovering human magic or simply filling roles?
> - How can you add meaningful human connection to the service you provide to your guests?
> - How would Super Skills like empathy, kindness, curiosity, and creativity enhance your brand?

2
Human Connection: The Hidden Pulse Of Your Competitive Advantage

R ight now, your mind should be whispering: *If I ignore this, am I losing money?* and *How is it relevant?*

Ignoring this would indeed make you lose money. Connection is currency that many hospitality businesses burn through without realising.

Let's be clear – the pace of change is relentless. Daily shifting expectations and a shortage of talented individuals are business as usual. With technology rapidly advancing, the desire for authentic human connection only increases.

The importance of human connection

Human connection is the hidden pulse of hospitality. Each beat injects life and rhythm into your operation, driving revenue and profit. Its life force makes the difference between your property being a pit stop or a pilgrimage.

Your challenge? Win their hearts. Take their breath away. Become their one and only. How? Simply meeting service standards will not be enough. The way forwards is in creating a culture of connection alchemy, enhanced by your team's skills and by human magic.

Connection is not a soft skill. It is a power move that:

- Inspires your team to create experiences aligned with your values
- Turns guests into lifelong devotees
- Creates loyalty and belonging
- Elevates your brand into a beloved icon

If you do not make a move, someone else will worm their way into your guests' hearts. Competitors may either steal them or poach your top employees.

The rewards of human connection

When employees have the freedom to blend technical excellence with intuitive improvisation, they create delightful, unexpected moments that transform service into emotional touchpoints. When team members collaborate, their efforts and energy create genuine connections that can transform the mundane into moments that matter, making an immeasurable positive impact on the business. You can start to build a place that both guests and employees want to stay at, belong to, and commit to. That is the real power of authentic hospitality.

The cost of neglect

Ignore the need for human connection, and your hotel becomes another forgettable option in a sea of sameness. Guests reduce you to a transaction. Employees treat working for you as a straightforward job (for now). You are rated on convenience instead of connection. Price becomes the only deciding factor. What values message does your brand signal? Transactional. Quittable. Forgettable. Replaceable.

The Lost Kitchen case study: A love letter to human connection

The Lost Kitchen in Freedom, Maine, is an icon of innovative, authentic human connection. Founded in 2014 by chef and hospitality maverick Erin French, this small, renowned restaurant completely reimagined the reservation process. By understanding something crucial that the rest of the industry had forgotten, it gained a cult following as a food and hospitality destination.

The postcard revolution

In 2018 Erin flipped the script on reservations. Gone were the point-and-click systems. Instead, hopeful diners mailed in a handwritten postcard, complete with real stamps, ink, and effort (Calderone, 2023).

Thousands of postcards poured in, each one a miniature love letter offering glimpses into people's lives: heartfelt stories, hand-drawn sketches, even glitter (reportedly, Erin's team is still vacuuming). Booking a reservation became more than luck and speed. It was a shared ritual, an emotional investment, and a powerful act of human connection.

People loved it.

The ROI of realness

The Lost Kitchen turned the reservation itself into a meaningful milestone event. Before diners even set foot inside, they were emotionally connected, their anticipation part of the overall experience. Instead of faceless names in a booking, the restaurant team read personal stories, celebrations, and dreams of future guests. These tiny gestures of humanity sowed the seeds for a personalised, intuitive, and warm home-style service.

Remarkably, business did not decline with the added friction in the reservation process. It soared. The slow build of anticipation had become a delightful part of the hospitality experience. When something feels rare and special, it becomes irresistible and worth the wait.

Why efficiency isn't the (only) answer

There is no denying that efficiency keeps the wheels turning – rooms are cleaned, rubbish is collected, and plumbing works – all in line with standards, operating procedures, and industry best practices.

Come on, though – let us be honest – has anyone ever written a five-star review about how efficiently their sheets were laundered or how well their toilet flushed? No.

Guests gush about how your team made them feel. The warm welcome, the unexpected kindness, the service recoveries, and the unscripted moments that left them feeling seen, valued, and cherished. This is the ROI of realness, where efficiency, emotion, ingenuity, and authenticity work in harmony with care to turn ordinary service into unforgettable memories.

Efficiency and exacting service are not enough if you want your property to be desired rather than simply booked. You must prioritise human connection and commit to building a brand that both guests and employees fall in love with. Ignore this, and your hotel becomes another forgettable option in a sea of sameness.

Booking a hotel room or reserving a table at many restaurants can feel like undergoing root canal work. The hospitality industry's obsession with efficiency has stripped away anticipation, reducing bookings to joyless transactions and wait-list purgatory.

Thousands once vied digitally for The Lost Kitchen's forty seats, turning excitement into stress. Faced with this, the restaurant had two choices:

- Automate and digitise
- Do something radically different and unexpected

They chose the second, sparking a quiet rebellion with simple postcards.

It worked like magic.

The industry's deep-rooted fallacy around friction

Conventional business wisdom tells us that friction is bad, encouraging the push for fewer clicks, faster processes, and easy convenience.

What if removing friction removes meaning, though?

Psychology proves that effort increases perceived value. The harder something is to acquire, the more we desire it. In the hospitality industry, though, the trend continues towards more automation, digitisation, and operational efficiency, squeezing out a place for personal touch.

Scarcity, when approached with respect, attentiveness, and customer care in mind, creates wholesome desire.

Erin French understood that her restaurant's success lay not in removing effort but in creating desire, slowly, one person at a time.

Are you selling convenience or creating desire?

Ease is overrated. The most memorable experiences are not created by efficient service delivery; they are earned.

Had The Lost Kitchen automated reservations, it would have joined countless restaurants with impersonal, stressful digital queues. Instead, postcards transformed the booking process into a meaningful story and a ritual that stirred excitement and a desire to belong. The business side effect? Genuine marketing gold.

If you chase only clickable convenience, your brand will not be remembered once the transaction ends. The real magic doesn't come from removing effort. It comes from making the effort meaningful and the experience worth the wait for the people who matter.

That is priceless!

Why authentic hospitality is about more than well-trained service

At a time when Caribbean resorts often fell into predictable categories – bikinis at the pool bars or jackets on the terrace for pre-dinner sundowners – the region's original allure of effortless elegance seemed lost.

Carlisle Bay offered something different. The partnership between Pat Doherty (Harcourt Developments) and Gordon Campbell Gray (One Aldwych, London) redefined boutique luxury in the Caribbean.

In 2003 Carlisle Bay reemerged on Antigua's south coast, minimalist, sophisticated, and intentionally rebellious against the typical riot of tropical clichés. Carlisle Bay pioneered a particular brand of 'barefoot chic' with a heartbeat, and independent luxury that was confidently effortless and unapologetically laid-back.

However, Carlisle Bay's real revolution was not its contemporary design, spa, forty-five-seat screening room, or curated library. It was its people and the reimagining of a luxury boutique hospitality experience, led and brought to life by its team.

Vision and culture DNA notes infused into the opening team recruitment

Right from the start, the resort had a clear vision and a bold declaration:

- We will create 'the ultimate snob-free, chilled-out experience'.
- Technology will never replace the human touch.
- VIP hierarchies are eliminated – all guests and employees are equal but have different responsibilities.
- We all do luggage – from bell captain to general manager – no exceptions.

- Standards matter, but service is a philosophy about *presence*, not protocol.

- Timeless hospitality principles must be lived, not languishing in the employee handbook.

- Team members are trusted, guided, and empowered to create connection.

This became the opening team's DNA: 237 carefully chosen employees delivered a signature guest experience that was intuitive, passionate, effortless, and deeply personalised.

Industry awards and accolades followed by the boatload. Competitors tried to copy the approach, but none could replicate it, because what Carlisle Bay created was not scripted; it was lived and experienced by every employee and guest, every day.

What follows is a parable. To respect privacy, the names of guests and team members are fictional, and stories have been blended. The moments described are an amalgam of many real interactions and experiences that defined Carlisle Bay's opening years. They are shared here not to spotlight individuals, but to illuminate the cultural DNA that made the resort's hospitality truly unforgettable. These composite vignettes capture the essence of how the resort team turned service into something richer: hospitality with a heartbeat.

From checklists to chicken soup: The Carlisle Bay parable

It was a balmy, breezy Tuesday afternoon in November when Mr and Mrs Davis arrived. Mrs Davis glided into the lobby, stylish but tense. Mr Davis trailed behind, rumpled and miserable, losing a battle with a brutal head cold that had been worsened by the long flight from London.

At the front desk, Sam was ready. Greetings and introductions were warm, with no unnecessary chit-chat. The check-in was smooth. Preferences were confirmed. Get-well wishes were genuine.

The Davis couple were then whisked to their suite after a flawless, frictionless process. The guest check-in SOP was executed perfectly, as trained, with competent efficiency after calm, unobtrusive assessment of the situation.

However, the story did not end there. Sam's role was not just to deliver the standard; her calling was to *care*.

The Carlisle Bay question

Sam carried a secret weapon – an aide-mémoire embedded in the resort's culture and known to each team member: *How can I provide love, care, and warmth to my guests and colleagues?* Not: *How do I check them in quickly?* Or: *How do I hit my KPIs?*

The Carlisle Bay question served as a guide that prompted a mindset: read the mood. Feel the moment. Then act.

Sam picked up the phone to her colleagues looking after food and beverage (F&B). The kitchen prepared two bowls of house-made chicken soup, with hot pepper sauce on the side. Room service expedited delivery. This was accompanied by a handwritten note: 'I hope you feel better soon. This will help. Not as good as my grandma's, but close. Get well, Sam.'

A gentle knock later, and the Davises' surprise melted into gratitude. The team had delivered a hug in a bowl, served with a note that created connection and shared an experience of authentic, remarkable hospitality.

It took many hearts and hands – not just a lone rock star or genius employee – to create this meaningful, memorable experience. Authentic hospitality is a team endeavour that involves seamless service combined with intuitive, unscripted care delivered by emotionally intelligent, skilled team members with the autonomy to act with heart.

The cost to the resort? Two bowls of soup.

Did Sam need permission? No.

What did it create? A guest experience that no competitor or algorithm could replicate.

Two bowls of soup became an unforgettable moment radiating empathy, kindness, and care. Checklists are an excellent aid for efficient, smooth operation, but they do not create an emotional connection. People do.

Sam was not simply executing SOPs; she was creating meaningful experiences by improvising alongside her fellow connection makers. The Carlisle Bay question was not an empty slogan or marketing gimmick. It was a thinking, feeling, and acting guide that no service script can capture.

The real secret to consistently creating this kind of genuine hospitality? It begins with who you hire.

Danny Meyer: Hire for hospitality quotient (HQ)

Danny Meyer, founder of Union Square Hospitality Group, shares, hospitality is almost impossible to teach. It's all about hiring the right people with a high hospitality quotient. He defines HQ as the degree to which you are happier yourself when you make someone else feel better. It has everything to do with what your motivations are behind the amazing technical skills you have (Farnam Street, 2021).

Meyer hires for both technical skill (needed for doing the function of the job, eg making sushi or a Negroni) and HQ (emotional skills like kindness, optimism, curiosity, work ethic, empathy, self-awareness, and integrity). Technical skills can be taught, but what is essential for what he calls *enlightened hospitality* comes from his employees' HQ (Meyer, 2006).

Are you hiring for human magic or compliant competence?

Competence matters. Guests expect precision. If you believe technical skill is enough, though, you are mistaken, and you are shortchanging your guests and your business.

The moments that amaze are rarely the ones guests expect; they are the ones guests never saw coming and could not have imagined. They are moments created by a master team of connection makers who have the freedom and agency to sense, feel, and act.

Now, imagine the impact of your brand if every employee on your team were a hospitality alchemist. That is your signature brand flavour that competitors cannot copy.

Are you hiring them? If not, someone else will.

This guide shows you how.

> **REFLECTION PROMPTS**
> - What delightfully inefficient yet unique human rituals can you introduce to transform your guest experience into moments that matter to both your team and your guests?
> - Does your team culture and brand experience generate stories worth sharing?
> - Are your employees free to read the moment and act without needing to ask permission?
> - Do they create real connections while getting tasks done in the correct way?

3
Overview Of The Unorthodox Interviewer's Guide

Ideally, you will choose your team members with more care than you do the thread count of your hotel's bed liners. Just as you are particular about the provenance of the produce for your restaurant, you will be equally discerning about each team member's background and potential. Your commitment to crafting your work culture will match your insistence on using the finest ingredients for your kitchen's sustainably sourced, six-grain artisan bread, made daily from scratch.

This isn't idealism. It is a bold, innovative, strategic move that is proven to work. Case in point: The PIG Hotels.

The success of PIG

Beginning in 2011, Robin and Judy Hutson revolutionised a niche in UK hospitality when they launched The PIG Hotels, a collection of luxury boutique hotels celebrated not only for refined comfort but also for making culture a signature brand ingredient. Robin, a pioneering hotelier, was determined from day one never to sacrifice authenticity for accolades or to scale for its own sake. Growth decisions must pass what they call the Darling Test – expansion happens only if it preserves principles, story, and the special magic that makes guests say, 'Darling, let's go to The Pig'. If the answer isn't an enthusiastic yes, the location is off the table (Boutique Hotelier, 2023b).

However, the secret sauce behind The PIG's phenomenal success is more than the hotels' sumptuous interiors or the values that show up in every aspect of the operation: kitchen gardens that feed the menu, suppliers chosen with integrity, and the stunning historic buildings that honour the land and community in which they are located.

The real secret is the people. Former CEO Tom Ross emphasises the power of genuine hospitality: 'Energetic staff members who give personable, authentic service and who really buy into the brand are the backbone to The Pig's success' (Boutique

Hotelier, 2023b). Rather than polished perfection, Ross chooses passion and character, preferring 'an energetic eighteen-year-old who loves what they do' over an experienced hire lacking enthusiasm.

Their squad are celebrated as hosts, not just staff. 'We have this thing called the extra 5% in the spirit of generosity. .. Whether or not it's your first time carrying a tray and speaking to someone, you want to do it in the right way and be nice and genuine,' Ross explains (Boutique Hotelier, 2023b).

This bold, human-led strategy pays off. Guests consistently rave about the authenticity and warmth they experience, resulting in a fiercely loyal community and exemplary thriving hospitality brand that teams stay with, and which industry peers admire and envy.

If you employ a similar strategy, you are in good company. Like the PIG Hotel leaders, you reject the notion that creating a cookie-cutter culture is the path to success. Above all, you are tired of trading values for profit and grabbing more for the sake of it.

As Robin Hutson puts it bluntly, 'I have always believed that the barriers to business success are not the often given reasons of market conditions, […] it's much more likely to be the inability to build the right team around you' (Boutique Hotelier, 2023a).

This guide is not for everyone (and that is the point)

Picture this: You do not play by the old rules. You set the pace and lead by challenging stale beliefs about how to operate a hospitality business. While others prioritise guest service scores, industry awards, and intend-to-recommend ratings above all else, you trust your employees and put them at the centre of your human-led hospitality business.

Conventional wisdom will tell you to stick to what is tried and tested. Play it safe. Don't give in. Tried and tested is no match for today's challenges, though. Safe and predictable approaches create a business that scales itself into sameness and oblivion. All this begs the question, Conventional best practices are best for whom?

Instead of playing it safe, you pose conscience-pricking questions others dodge:

- How can we settle when more human connection is needed?
- Is this [action, plan, or idea you are pondering] right for our guests, employees, culture, community, and the planet?

You have seen what happens when humanity is stripped from hospitality: numbed-down guest experiences, rote-learned service, and an overzealous trimming of the ooey-gooey, improbable, spontaneous human magic that makes your hospitality brand sing and stand out.

It is impossible to hire human magic using a standard HR recruitment playbook

Some hotels and restaurants are copies of copies, but let's say this doesn't apply to yours. Your property is not for everyone. You know your guests intimately. Now you must assemble a team that moves in harmony with your property's brand values and identity. You need an A-team of super-connectors who transform simple tasks and everyday interactions into moments of joy. You also need a proven interview framework to help you discover and hire those people.

Conventional recruitment practices are based on industrial-era people management models. They are great for assessing technical skills but inadequate for hiring human magic. The fact is your business needs both.

Overhauling your approach to recruitment and doing what most would dismiss as slightly bonkers is not risky; it is necessary. Doing things differently is how you stand out from the crowd. Like Simone Biles defying gravity, you will leave others baffled, muttering, *How did they do that?*

Changing your approach is an act of stubborn courage and a savvy business move suited to these shifting times. Remember, you started your company to do more than survive or to operate a profitable business. You dream of your business thriving and your team flourishing, and that team includes you.

This guide is just for you

Your current reality might be like this: Faced with limited fresh alternatives, you are relying on policy manuals and interview templates that yield stock answers. You are stuck on the hiring hamster wheel, with your operation revving like a Ferrari with the handbrake on.

It's time to get off the merry-go-round and look for a better way. Yes, there is an alternative way to recruit hospitality alchemists. There is even better news – it is backed by science and field-tested.

Your future awaits.

Here is the deal. It requires you to:

- Let go of old hiring models and interviewing mindsets
- Embrace a radically different approach
- Break free from hiring by generic, outdated person specifications

OVERVIEW OF THE UNORTHODOX INTERVIEWER'S GUIDE

If you are looking for more best practices, you are in the wrong place

This is not your typical HR hiring manual. There is no list of pre-authorised interview questions and a tidy stack of policies and standard forms. Instead, this unorthodox interviewer's guide is part manifesto and part GPS coordinates. Designed for rule breakers and maverick hospitality leaders, it offers an imaginative framework grounded in real-world pragmatism.

Why? Because so-called best practices were built for efficiency, not enchantment. They prioritise consistency over connection and technical proficiency over humanity.

The limits of the traditional interview

Standard hiring processes are designed to fill positions fast with two types of interviews:

- **Competency-based interviews.** These are great for assessing technical ability but poor at revealing character.

- **Behavioural interviews.** These are good for past stories but bad for predicting real-time emotional agility.

If you are not paying close attention, these interviews allow compliant clones and fool's gold candidates to slip into your operation and colonise your culture. We have all had this experience. You will no doubt have hired candidates who looked perfect on paper, only to realise that they were all polish and no presence, pizzazz with no passion.

Let's put an end to that. You cannot hire human magic using standard scripts, checklists, and interrogations. You must go beyond those.

Introducing Human Magic Hiring

This is not a formula or a hack. It is a flexible approach that:

- Uses a structure, not a straitjacket, to guide deeper, more authentic connection with your candidates
- Poses bold, surprising questions that uncover Super Skills and the capacity to create magic
- Focuses on human contributors, not unicorns or any other mythically perfect hires
- Treats interviews like supper clubs, not interrogations

Human Magic Hiring, when done right, mirrors your guests' experience of your hospitality. The most revealing interviews do not feel like interviews; they are story-sharing moments and exchanges that feel like effortless conversations. Human Magic Hiring is an invitation to adopt a more advanced, hospitality-led approach to interviewing, where candidates are hosted, not grilled.

The Three-Course Conversation interview framework

This menu forms the basis for the Human Magic Hiring approach to interviews:

- **Appetiser** – starter questions to reveal instincts and personality

- **Entrée** – core questions to explore the candidate's understory, based on the ten Super Skills

- **Dessert** – prompt questions to reveal hospitality, purpose, and cultural alignment

The mission: By the end of the interview, you should understand not only what the candidates can do but also who they are. Here are the ten human qualities – the ten Super Skills – you must explore to discover the true person behind the professional persona:

1. **Empathy** – intuitively sensing and responding meaningfully to others

2. **Kindness** – radiating genuine warmth and thoughtful care

3. **Curiosity** – enjoying an exploratory, questioning mindset

4. **Creativity** – improvising and solving problems imaginatively

5. **Unlearn learning** – letting go of the obsolete and embracing the new

6. **Gratitude** – expressing appreciation with meaning and generosity

7. **Vulnerability** – being open and authentic

8. **Courage** – boldly acting beyond conventional thinking and the status quo

9. **Resilience** – maintaining grace under pressure, with the ability to bounce back and bounce forwards

10. **Purpose connection** – aligning personal values and motivation with the organisation's vision and mission

The science behind Human Magic Hiring

This is not hocus pocus.

While conducting my own field research, following my intuition (also known as my Super Skills spidey sense), I indulged my penchant for rule-breaking by going off script during interviews, teasing out stories, making uncommon connections … only to discover that there was supporting empirical evidence. Rebellion vindicated and validated.

The Human Magic Hiring approach, including the Three-Course Conversation interview framework, draws on validated research from organisational psychology, emotional intelligence, and behavioural science, as well as the work of doctors such as Brené Brown (https://brenebrown.com/about), Vikki Barnes (www.drvikkibarnes.com/about), Adam Grant (https://adamgrant.net/about/biography), and Todd Kashdan (https://toddkashdan.com/about), among others. The published research findings inspired me to adapt these insights to HR discipline and formalise the design of this ALT-HR hiring guide.

Tips for the Three-Course Conversation interview framework

Here are three quick interviewing style tips for the considerate host

- **Be curious, not clever.** Let your questions invite, not interrogate.
- **Let silence linger.** Reflection takes time.
- **Capture the nuance.** Remain alert, open, and observant, taking field notes like a cultural anthropologist.

Human Magic Hiring is not about hiring perfection. It is about spotting brilliance and the probability of any candidate making a valuable contribution. It is about understanding their self-worth and their potential for development.

Let's assemble your dream team with science and a dash of rebellion

Upcoming chapters will show you how to:

- Identify and interview for the ten Super Skills
- Use sixty-plus powerful questions to uncover true character and potential for human magic
- Spot red flags and hidden signals to be on the lookout for (BOLOs)
- Create an interview experience that reflects your hospitality, guests, and employer brand

Human Magic Hiring goes beyond selecting employees who can perform an operational job. When you focus on adding Super Skills to your team's technical know-how, you create a complex competency and culture cocktail that becomes a distinctive brand advantage your competitors cannot copy.

Are you ready? Let's start shaking and stirring things up.

OVERVIEW OF THE UNORTHODOX INTERVIEWER'S GUIDE

> **REFLECTION PROMPTS**
> - What outdated hiring practices are being used in your business? How is that working for you?
> - Are you recruiting for polish or for pizzazz, technical skills or values, presence or passion?
> - Which of the ten Super Skills are missing on your team right now?

PART TWO
THE WHAT

4
Spec'd To Fail: What You Lose When You Hire By The Book

Let's think first about how traditional person specifications – hereafter referred to as person spec – cost you magic. When you hire by the book, you fixate on the details, scrutinising spreadsheets, the equipment, the technology systems, and the assets. You refine experiences to the finest detail, fretting over the décor, the menu, service standards, and signature accents. You never build or renovate your property without precise, up-to-date blueprints, and plans for the structure and interior design.

This begs the question: Why is your culture and employer brand shaped by generic best practices, outdated job descriptions, and antiquated person specs? The approach is like relying on flawed plans or trusting architects who lack a thorough understanding of hospitality operations to design your restaurant or build your hotel, all while hoping for a safe and sturdy structure.

The problem with hiring to the person spec

You are likely familiar with the person spec box in job descriptions, which typically contains a concise list of required qualifications, experience, and technical skills. A well-written person spec may meet legal contracting requirements, serving as insurance against obvious hiring mistakes. However, person specs can also turn into bear traps.

Most job descriptions do not define excellence or what extraordinary contribution looks like. They provide a checklist of basic competencies to be satisfied and minimum requirements to be met, with the better ones listing core company values. You might be wondering what is wrong with hiring based on this checklist, and the answer is nothing at all, if your goal is to hire for only minimum requirements and satisfactory standards. You only get exactly what is specified in the job description – nothing more, the same as everyone else, served cold.

Now, I imagine that you are in the business of delivering more than well-marketed mediocrity, instead creating something extraordinary. In that case, you need to consider the largely undefined critical criteria not captured in the usual person spec.

Here are some examples to help you appreciate the difference:

- A chef can make a dish by following a recipe, but can they turn a guest's craving into an off-menu masterpiece?
- A front desk assistant can check a guest in efficiently, but do they know when to break protocol to create a memorable moment?
- A server can deliver a meal to a table, but can they also read the unspoken cues that transform service into a magical experience?
- A maintenance technician can fix the leaking faucet, but do they care enough to check the room and replace a blown bulb before they leave?

Typical job descriptions outline *minimum* expectations and signal to employees the standards they must meet. It sets the bar low. An employee who meets the person spec and does not work beyond the job description will not transform guests into advocates or help build a standout team. Even with good effort and satisfactory performance, as prescribed, they will not deliver exceptional service or the wow guest experience you want your property to be known for. This establishes low standards in your team's mindset, in your culture and operational systems, and in the overall experience your guests encounter.

As Seth Godin reminds us (Godin, 2018 and 2020), instead of aiming merely to 'meet spec', for us, the real opportunity is to go beyond the minimum and bring humanity to the work. Specifications are industrial tools; they keep your team compliant, but never create delight. Godin argues that if all you offer is box-ticking service delivered by compliant cogs, a machine or an algorithm will likely do it faster and cheaper. What makes people indispensable, your guest experience priceless, and your hospitality unforgettable is the human edge: the care, improvisation, and connection that no job description can fully capture.

Hiring to meet specs will not make your hospitality brand remarkable. It will make it easily copyable and hold it back from achieving greatness. This is because technical skills can be taught, but human magic lies hidden in the human attributes of each employee you hire, waiting to be revealed. Depending on traditional interviews alone will not help you find the special qualities needed for authentic human connection and genuine hospitality. They give you:

- Employees who meet standard job requirements
- Service providers instead of storytellers
- A team that is technically capable but emotionally unremarkable

The uniquely human qualities you need to find cannot be taught; they must be uncovered and given room to soar. Natural hosting instincts, innate care, and intuitive connection skills are often found in the most unexpected places. This guide will show you exactly where to look.

The businesses that survive, thrive, and elevate hospitality do not just 'meet spec' – they rewrite the criteria entirely.

Beware: The hidden cost of hiring the wrong people

A bad hire is infinitely more dangerous than a frustrating inconvenience. It is a hazardous, unseen leak in your business that:

- Corrodes culture from within
- Zaps the team of its energy
- Commoditises guests into 'just another booking'
- Gnaws away at trust and morale, one lacklustre interaction at a time
- Erodes revenue and potential profits

The cumulative effect of a bad hire is the slow, silent drain on your investment, your culture, and the hospitality dream you are building.

The most dangerous part is that you may not realise the damage until it is too late. Guests rarely complain about mediocrity; they simply do not return, and they spread the word about their substandard experience. Meanwhile, team members often stay silent about toxic leaders and co-workers until they withdraw commitment or quit.

Persistent service failures and indifferent guest experiences will be a drain on your coffers and damage your brand reputation. Ask any hotelier or restaurateur about the cost of 'comping' – compensating guests when the team drops the ball and leadership is lacking.

Each day you sleepwalk through hiring, relying on outdated recruitment policies, you risk choosing someone who looks good on paper and aces the interview but causes chaos in practice. You must remain vigilant!

Four types that will slowly suck your property's magic dry

Some hires are obvious disasters from day one; those are the easy ones to spot. Others are the slow, silent wrecking balls to watch out for. It can take months or even years for their true character and the lethal impact on your operation to be revealed. Undetected, these employees set about creating mischief and mayhem in your team, culture, and guest experience and, ultimately, on the bottom line.

With over twenty years' experience in hospitality hiring, I've identified the repeat offenders and added them to my Recruitment Rogues Gallery. Here are four primary types to spot and stay clear of:

1. The fool's gold find
2. The institutional parrot
3. The mimic
4. The jobsworth

1. The fool's-gold find

The fool's-gold find shines in the interview: slick, polished, charming.

They have the perfect CV, crammed with credentials, experience in the 'right' companies, and a glossy social media profile featuring inspirational quotes and humblebrag posts. They interview with polish, charm, and all the right answers. They arrive with glowing references, drop names (mentioning all the right ones), and give charming answers. However, when you ask questions about their experiences that require thinking beyond the obvious, they are at a loss. As you dig further beneath the surface, what do you discover? No instinct. No depth. No natural spark. No magic.

This candidate type shines on paper until you realise it is all glitter and not gold.

2. The institutional parrot

The institutional parrot talks the theory but cannot walk it in practice.

They recite policies, quote best practices, regurgitate industry lingo, and share past case studies as if they have lived them. When you probe deeper, though, into how precisely they applied or adapted these principles in real-life operations, suspicious holes begin to appear in their stories.

They lack the empathy, creativity, courage to execute, and the adaptability needed to improvise in fluid or high-stakes situations.

3. The mimic

A master borrower of others' success, the mimic does not create; they copy.

They boast, talking up 'their' achievements, but rarely, if at all, have they done the work. They contribute little that is original and ride the energy tailwinds of your top performers until resentment grows within the team.

They gobble up team morale to fuel their steady climb up the organisation, rising through the ranks, leaving waves of frustration in their wake.

4. The jobsworth

This term comes from British slang, referring to someone who responds to work requests with, *I can't do that; it's more than my job's worth.*

You know the type. They dodge additional work, resist learning, and duck helping others beyond their role spec. Unusual guest request? *Not my department.* Teammates need support? *My shift is over.* Opportunity to learn something new? *Not in my job description!* Requests for new ideas? *Above my pay grade.*

Rules are their refuge. Initiative is their enemy. They don't destroy overnight; they cement mediocrity by slowly dampening the spirit to care. Over time their mindset and behaviour snuff out your team's spark and blunt your competitive edge, one rule at a time.

The antidote

What if job descriptions in your company looked different? Imagine hiring for these qualities:

- Must have a sixth sense for knowing what a guest needs before they say a word
- Must find joy in making someone's day

- Must relish the challenge of transforming raw moments into hospitality magic
- Must believe that hospitality is more than service; it is an art form

Would you get fewer applicants? Possibly. Would you get better ones? Absolutely.

That is the shift needed.

The hard questions you need to ask

Consider these two options:

1. Hiring another 'meets-the-spec' employee and hoping that they will bring more than the minimum standard
2. Taking a chance on a candidate with the right instincts and an unconventional background

The first path leads to mediocrity. The second leads to magic. Which path will you choose?

Human magic is where connection, heartfelt hospitality, and real brand difference reside. Human Magic Hiring is vital for assembling a team of remarkable hospitality alchemists.

REFLECTION PROMPTS

- How can you redesign your job descriptions to make sure you catch the all-important Super Skills?
- Are you willing to take a chance on an off-spec candidate with the right instincts and an unconventional background?
- Are you accidentally letting any fool's gold finds, institutional parrots, mimics, or jobsworths slip through your hiring process?

5
The Anatomy Of A Hospitality Alchemist

If the last chapter gave you nightmares about the wrong hires, this one will restore your peace of mind. It will give you your treasure map, your BOLO (be on the lookout) guide, leading you to the team members you have been dreaming of.

Uncommon pairings

Niki Segnit's *The Flavour Thesaurus* (Segnit, 2010), beautifully captures the paradox of pairing the unexpected, transporting readers on a sensory adventure to over a thousand possible flavour combinations. You could do worse than be inspired by her unconventional approach as you assemble a team of individuals ready to create the extraordinary.

Segnit's pairings include white chocolate with olives, beetroot with coconut, chicken with rose, and vanilla with shellfish. At first glance the combinations may seem illogical. However, surprisingly, the unexpected fusion amplifies each element, resulting in a completely new flavour profile and experience that neither ingredient could achieve on its own.

When something is unfamiliar, our first reaction might be to reject it, but diverse perspectives and embracing the unfamiliar can bring unexpected joy and innovation. Sometimes they serve us a generous portion of humble pie when we realise what we have missed out on by believing our assumptions to be facts.

If one area of hospitality can embrace daring culinary adventures, why not take the same courageous, experimental approach to hiring?

There is an undeniable paradoxical tension when you hire for the human magic that makes transformation in your team and guest experiences possible. When you do, you will feel a sense you cannot quite describe but instinctively recognise as magic bubbling.

You need to look to hire hospitality alchemists with a rare combination of technical skills and natural human qualities, like those in the ten Super Skills. Just as pairing Bollinger champagne with crispy fried chicken combines luxury and comfort, hospitality alchemists blend human efficiency and magic, creating a unique culture, where the irresistible, one-of-a-kind guest experience becomes the norm.

From commodified spec 'fits' to artisanal alchemist finds

Comfort zones feel safe and sensible. In a shifting business landscape, safe hiring delivers the predictable and entirely unremarkable. If hiring for cultural fit is your comfort zone, hiring for cultural amplification is your magic zone.

Human Magic Hiring might feel risky. The real risk, though, is that your brand is written off as ordinary, invisible, and replaceable in the hearts and minds of your guests and employees and within your market niche.

Hospitality alchemists do not slot neatly into conventional job specs. They create an entirely new category. Their gifts include:

- Making connections and magic from unscripted moments
- Sharing original perspectives and unexpected creativity that transform transactional service into transformational experiences

- Bringing agency and courage to rewrite the rules to suit fluid situations when SOPs fall short

- Adding resilience to your brand and agility to your operation, thanks to their comfort with unpredictability

Hiring hospitality alchemists demands a shift in mindset, not another recruitment method. I'll now show you how to spot, hire, and set them free to fire up your operation, supercharge your team, and enhance your guest experience offerings.

The anatomy of a hospitality alchemist

Hospitality alchemists excel at blending technical skills with Super Skills for maximum human connection. Where others see issues, they spot opportunities and take action. They craft shared stories with guests and colleagues, rather than blindly sticking to service scripts and standards. You cannot fully recognise these impressive qualities from a CV or LinkedIn profile; they are best identified during an interview designed specifically to discover them.

To help you prepare for your quest, let's look at a snapshot of a BOLO guide with sample interview questions to help you spot and hire different types of hospitality alchemists.

BOLO examples

BOLO #1: Indispensable connectors

Indispensable connectors are like linchpins. In Seth Godin's words: 'The indispensable employee brings humanity and connection and art to her organization. She is the key player, the one who is difficult to live without, the person you can build something around' (Godin, 2010).

Indispensable connectors do not just fit in; they stand out. They challenge stale thinking, push for continuous improvement, and craft 'an emotional point of difference' (Jiwa, 2014) that guests rave about.

> **(?) Sample interview question**
>
> What's one unique contribution you have made to a team or guest experience that was not part of your job description?

BOLO #2: Intuitive improvisers

Like neo-generalists, intuitive improvisers are adaptable and fluid individuals who blend specialist expertise with generalist knowledge. They rise to the challenge to create new insights, while thriving in shifting contexts (Mikkelsen and Martin, 2016).

Think about the world's best mixologists: part chemist, part therapist, part performer. They read the room, not just the recipe rules.

 Sample interview question

> Tell me about a situation where you turned a guest's frustration into a memorable positive experience.

BOLO #3: Imaginative hosts

Like the dream weavers who practise transforming the mundane into the memorable, imaginative hosts turn ordinary service moments into 'you've got to see this' experiences (Guidara, 2022).

This is like the Carlisle Bay chicken soup story, where an intuitive front desk assistant sensed a guest needed comfort, not just cuisine, and tag-teamed with her colleagues to create something unforgettable.

 Sample interview question

> Tell me about a time you went off script to deliver something to a guest that they didn't ask for but clearly needed.

Technician + magician = alchemist

Hiring for alchemy means placing a calculated bet on human connection and your team. If your current hiring process does not scare you, just a little, you are playing it too safe.

Hire hospitality alchemists and trade:

- Predictability for innovation
- Soulless transactions for connections that matter
- Ordinary stays for a sense of belonging

This is not just theory; it is a deep, disciplined practice. Extraordinary experiences do not come from predictable processes. They come from giving people the autonomy and freedom to wield their magic in their daily interactions and work.

Hiring debate: Food as fuel vs nourishment

Safe hiring is like fast food – quick, convenient, efficient, adequate, but seldom memorable. Interviewing for human magic is like slow food – artful, hand-crafted, intentional, indulgent, and unforgettable.

What will you do? Play it safe by sticking to the same old standards; or reach for stories that connect and the Super Skills most overlook, and create the kind of hospitality that guests and team members will never forget?

Your move.

> **REFLECTION PROMPTS**
> - Are your interviews transactional or transformative?
> - Do you have the right mix of magicians and technicians?
> - Is your operational culture ready for a team of hospitality alchemists?

6
Alchemy By Numbers: The Skills You Can't Train But Must Find

Interviewing solely for job-related skills and career experience is like serving an unseasoned three-course meal. It will be technically edible but bland and quickly forgotten – out of sight and out of mind, like the crusty remnants of a room service tray left in the corridor overnight. Similarly, hospitality without the fizz of human connection is like champagne without bubbles – flat, disappointing, forgettable, and best poured down the sink.

Exceptional, one-of-a-kind, authentic hospitality that guests rave about requires more than skills that can be trained. It demands the essential ingredients of human magic.

Let us gather those ingredients.

The mirepoix in the secret sauce of hospitality alchemy

Just as a mirepoix blends finely chopped aromatic vegetables to give soups, stews, and sauces their subtle depth (Spencer, 2025), hospitality alchemy relies on the essential human ingredients found in the richness of a candidate's character and lived experiences.

Every human possesses these attributes, regardless of national origin, race, gender, social standing, political beliefs, or religious affiliation.

In practical hospitality terms, guests instinctively notice and are drawn to the human qualities that differentiate standard service from extraordinary experiences. Sadly, those qualities are often dimmed and rarely felt in most workplace cultures and daily operations.

The importance of the ten Super Skills

We have identified the ten innate human qualities that are the source of a candidate's unique human magic (see Chapter 3 for the full list). Those qualities can be revealed, nurtured, and amplified but not taught. You will find evidence of them in a candidate's inner life compass (beliefs, values, mindset, and purpose) and tacit knowledge (practical wisdom earned through effort, adversity, personal genius, and natural talent).

These Super Skills create the distinctive aromatic base that adds depth and flavour to every interaction and form the essential toolkit for your hospitality alchemists.

Why ten?

A serving of ten Super Skills strikes a perfect balance between depth and practicality, making it ideal for creating human connections and extraordinary guest experiences. Ten is a sweet spot – more manageable than the eighty-seven emotions and experiences mapped by Brené Brown in *Atlas of the Heart* (2021); yet more comprehensive than Danny Meyer's six HQ traits: kindness and optimism, curiosity, work ethic, empathy, self-awareness, integrity (Farnam Street, 2021).

Focusing on ten Super Skills provides the perfect recipe for your signature hospitality blend.

From possibility to probability

Too often, hiring for human magic is perceived as something mystical and intangible – possible yet unreliable. This chapter invites you to move from the realm of possibility (*It might happen*) into probability (*It is likely to happen, if we design for it*).

Possibility is hopeful. Probability is powerful.

When you hire intentionally for human magic, with the right design and mindset, hospitality alchemy becomes not only possible but also provable, predictable, and practised. That shift – from dream to discipline – is where the alchemy resides.

The surprising maths of human magic

Hospitality done right feels like wizardry. We instantly recognise it when we feel it. Quantifying it, however, feels as elusive as catching wind with your hands. What if we distilled human magic into a compelling number – one that satisfies both romantics and spreadsheet enthusiasts?

Imagine a team of 250 hospitality alchemists. Each has ten Super Skills. Assume each alchemist draws on an average of three skills per guest interaction. This blend generates exactly 120 unique ways to enchant guests.

The hospitality alchemy formula components

- Ten Super Skills
- Three skills per interaction (aligning with the rule of three)
- 120 unique combinations per alchemist
- 250 alchemists = 30,000 moments of guest magic

Why three skills?

- Two skills lack depth.
- Four or more create cumbersome complexities.
- Three is balanced – memorable, intuitive, and emotionally impactful.

From fairy tales to cooking and advertising slogans, the number three possesses deep storytelling authority. As explained in Copyblogger (Clark, 2023): 'It all comes down to the way we humans process information. We have become proficient at pattern recognition by necessity, and three is the smallest number of elements required to create a pattern.' The rule of three makes information sticky, memorable, and satisfying.

The rule of three is not a quirk; it is a potent psychological tool. Hospitality alchemists who draw on three skills per interaction create a natural chemistry that guests remember.

Why 120 matters

That number may seem humble, yet it represents a significant number of:

- Distinct emotional guest interactions
- Stories that spark advocacy
- Moments remembered long after checkout

Authentic hospitality thrives on variety and surprise. One alchemist with 120 possible combinations holds a treasure chest of opportunities to amaze with intuitive artistry.*

Why 30,000 moments of guest magic?

One alchemist can provide 120 combinations, so a team of 250 gives you 30,000:

- 30,000 distinct guest connections
- 30,000 shareable moments
- 30,000 brand-building touchpoints

Pause and take that in: 30,000 unique opportunities to make guests fall in love with your property.

The maths made musical

If formulas leave your brain fried, try music. Western music is built on just seven notes: A, B, C, D, E, F, G. Yet from these, infinite masterpieces emerge.

---

* For the mathematically curious, to calculate combinations where number does not matter, the formula is $^nC_r = n! / (n-r)! \, r!$ (where C represents the number of combinations). In our illustration, n = 10 (total skills) and r = 3 (per interaction), so $^nC_r = 10! / (10-3)! \, 3! = 10! / 7! \, 3! = 120$.

Take *Beethoven × Beyoncé* by Steve Hackman (Hackman, no date) – a blend of Beethoven's *Ode to Joy* and Beyoncé's *Halo*. It is an audacious mashup that bridges classical and pop genres.

Listen to 'Bey-thoven' (Tsui, no date) – a fusion of the familiar and unfamiliar.

Now imagine your team as a musical ensemble. Ten Super Skills combined with technical expertise offer endless opportunities for harmony and improvisation.

Vanilla, orchids, and the art of hospitality alchemy

Creating a consistently enchanting guest experience is like hand-pollinating a vanilla orchid (Arefin, 2024). It requires intention, patience, and care, as well as a steady hand and a keen eye.

Vanilla orchids bloom for only one day. If left unattended, the probability of natural pollination is low. However, with a gentle hand, precise timing, and the right tools, a single flower transforms into a pod, and a pod becomes that flavour. Hospitality alchemy works the same way. Human magic is not random; it is intentional. It takes a singular culture, a leader who knows when to nurture and when to step back, and team members with agency and autonomy who can draw brilliance from unexpected situations.

It is slow work, rarely done, but worth it.

Why this maths matters

Rory Sutherland argues that real business impact lies in the unmeasurable elements such as the influence of stories compared with that of facts, in what he calls *psycho-logic* (Sutherland, 2019). Serving the expected maintains standards and upholds the status quo. Delivering the unexpected creates magic that makes a genuine hospitality experience both logically understood and emotionally felt. Imagine a bubbly champagne joy that is both nebulous and real at the same time. Human Magic Hiring commissions your in-house alchemists to transform ordinary transactions into unforgettable moments – and what leader doesn't want that for their business?

This chapter presents a counterpoint to conventional business beliefs, which tend to prize efficiency metrics and processes over intangibles. Human magic is the outlier that exists outside those norms. It is emotional because it touches how people feel, sparking joy, warmth, comfort, and belonging in ways no spreadsheet can capture. It is exponential, because one small act of unscripted care can multiply – delighting a guest, energising a team, and amplifying your reputation far beyond the original moment. Care and connection compounds; that's the beauty of alchemy in hospitality and an unmistakable source of your human-led edge.

Your alchemical invitation

If you have ever doubted prioritising human magic in hiring, here is your proof. Magic, it turns out, can be calculated, as illustrated above.

When you hire for magic, you build more than a workforce. You create a jazz ensemble of improvisation artists, creating riffs on staid sequences of service, transforming the ordinary into the extraordinary and enchanting both your guests and team. Now you do not just believe in human magic; you have the maths to prove it.

Are you ready to assemble your alchemical ensemble? It's time to shift from merely filling cold roles with warm bodies.

In the following chapter I'll cover how you can discover your next hospitality alchemist

---

REFLECTION PROMPTS

- Think of a recent lacklustre guest interaction. Which three Super Skills could have transformed it?
- Recall a standout hospitality experience. What three Super Skills were present?
- Analyse your top team members. Which Super Skills do they consistently use?
- Which Super Skills do you need more of in your team?

7
Interview Mise En Place: Prepare To Welcome Your Candidate

No professional chef worth their salt would dream of starting service without mise en place. Why should a masterful interviewer behave any differently?

The mise-en-place method

Imagine beginning your interview day in a flustered state. Notes scattered, hiring documents missing, questions vague, no structure, head spinning from distractions. Your candidate senses it all, and the connection fizzles before it can spark.

Be like a chef who never skips preparing ingredients and checking equipment before cooking. They understand the importance of having a system in place and the value of using it consistently to increase their chances of a smooth service.

Hiring is your first act of hospitality

Does your hiring process reflect or contradict your hospitality brand's value promise?

You would not serve an offensively salty, mealy dish to your guests. It would never leave the pass. Why, then, would you allow heavy-handed treatment during your recruitment experience?

Your hospitality begins before your candidate even enters the interview room. Perfunctory policies and processes are the reheated leftovers of tired, outmoded recruitment approaches. If you promise radically authentic and human-first hospitality, your hiring must embody that same spirit. This is not only about welcoming a strong candidate. It is also about extending grace as soon as it is determined that your business purpose and culture do not match with their aspirations, technical knowledge, and Super Skills range.

When you are clear about your culture and brand promise, ending the hiring journey early is fair, straightforward, and the right thing to do for both parties. Instead of a cold, inhospitable rejection letter or – worse – ghosting, kindly and firmly direct your candidate towards where their unique human magic will flourish. This is just the same as you would do with a guest who has found themselves in the wrong room or a hotel that does not suit their taste. Early offboarding is also an act of hospitality that honours your candidate's autonomy and agency in their job search, while preserving their dignity and your brand values.

When and why hiring becomes hosting:

- You are not just recruiting; you are telling your brand's story.

- You are not simply filling roles; you are shaping culture.

- You are not only onboarding staff; you are inviting alchemists to join in creating a legacy.

This is more than good business. It is a powerful business-building strategy in action.

Mental prep: A thirty-minute ritual

Fight the temptation to fly by the seat of your pants. Intentional prep brings clarity, calm, and confidence. A clear mise-en-place system allows space for authentic connection.

Calm and careful planning helps reduce interview mistakes and painful hiring choices such as the ones described in Chapter 4. When practised diligently, interview prep becomes a ritual, mentally preparing you to uncover your candidate's ten Super Skills and discover the next hospitality alchemist for your team.

Reframe the interview stage: The candidate is the hero

Traditional interviews position the company as the hero, with the candidate auditioning for a supporting role. Human Magic Hiring completely flips the script. Your candidate is the hero on a quest to use their skills, experiences, values, and voice in a meaningful way. You are not assessing a fit; you are inviting a contribution.

Your role becomes:

- Guide, not gatekeeper
- Story listener, not script reader
- Alchemist spotter, not checklist ticker

When you explore the intersection of your candidate's journey and your brand's purpose, and how joining your team can help them realise their dreams while fulfilling your company's vision, you unlock mutual flourishing.

Roll out the red carpet. Host them well.

Interview like a master truffle hunter

On my first long-haul flight after the pandemic, I skipped my usual in-flight entertainment of crime or action films. I instead became engrossed in a film about the dying art of traditional truffle hunting in Italy (Dweck and Kershaw, 2020). Deep in the forests of Piedmont, truffle hunters seek the elusive Alba truffle – a misshapen, earthy, rare, and prized delicacy.

Much like these truffle experts, you are not looking for common mushrooms (technical skills). You are hunting for truffles – ten priceless, innate Super Skills.

These include:

- Kindness that surfaces instinctively
- Courage that embraces vulnerability
- Empathy that lives in small, human gestures
- Unlearn learning deepened by passion and humility

Be vigilant. Each candidate possesses a unique Super Skills profile. These treasures live in the stories your candidate shares, for example, in tales of setbacks, triumphs, and good fortune. These are rich grounds where their human magic thrives. Together, they point to where their personal genius and natural talent shine.

Channel your inner sleuth by asking yourself:

- Do their stories ring true?
- Do their values align with their behaviours?
- Do they show natural, untrained brilliance?

Super Skills do not look remarkable on paper, but their subtle and transformative impact is unmistakable.

You are on a treasure hunt.

Set the stage for the magician to appear

To set the stage, you must adapt your hiring mindset and interview approach. Turn your interview into an adventure that explores human connection. Quick tip: Do not seek culture fits. Invite culture *amplifiers*.

To invite real magic to take the stage, you need to:

- Create trust and psychological safety
- Prioritise dialogue over interrogation
- Let curiosity lead; playful tangents may reveal gold
- Value passion and presence over pedigree
- Watch tone, body language, and energy

These actions create an environment where authentic stories flow, allowing Super Skills to rise to the surface and stay with you long after the interview ends.

Committing to human magic

Human Magic Hiring means:

- **Reflecting your brand values.** Your process is unmatched: memorable, meaningful, and magnetic.

- **Crafting culture, not just designing roles.** You hire for shared values, emotional resonance, agency, and autonomy.

- **Amplifying your brand difference.** Personalised, immersive, slow-style interviews reinforce your hospitality ethos and distinguish your employer brand.

- **Boosting retention.** People stay where their humanity is seen and their contributions are valued.

Still unsure about committing to Human Magic Hiring? Let's consider the rewards.

Three strategic benefits to your business

Here are just three of the main ways you stand to gain from Human Magic Hiring:

- **Stronger employer brand.** Candidates talk. When treated with care and dignity, they become ambassadors, creating a magnetic pull to other alchemists ideally suited to your business.
- **Superior guest experience.** Valued people deliver value to guests and colleagues, creating an infinite loop of authentic hospitality.
- **Enchanting, shareable interviews.** Your process becomes a story candidates love to tell – brand marketing gold.

We are living in a world obsessed with scrolling and scaling at speed, and full of uncertainties about AI domination. Step off the treadmill. Find your edge and brand distinction in something slow, sustainable, and human-led. Double down on creating and serving genuine value by investing in things that endure even in uncertain times such as human longing for connection, belonging, meaning, and stories that help us live our own hero's journey.

Human Magic Hiring is one way to help achieve this. When the uninitiated see your remarkable results and ask you, *How did you do that?*, cue your Mona Lisa smile and tell them, *It is human magic. You will know it when you feel it.*

Gatecrashers advisory: Sceptics and naysayers will show up uninvited

Of course, not everyone will get it. Some will scoff, reducing hiring to just logistics or a pipeline to optimise. Others, bearing the scars of past bad hiring decisions and still clutching on to outdated HR dogma, will mutter about 'fit' and sticking to what is tried and true. Tried, yes, but true now?

Let them be. Their scepticism says more about their experiences than about your instincts and vision. Treat it like background noise as you pioneer a more human, connected approach. Your job is not to persuade the non-believers or cajole anyone to join you.

Think of your decision like liquorice – delightfully intense, contentious, provocative, and, yes, divisive. Embrace that. You are not here to please everyone. You are here to assemble an extraordinary team whose magic cannot be cloned.

Yes, there will be challenges. However, it is far better to make bold, conscious hiring decisions than to play it safe and repeat the same uninspired patterns. Say yes to the new way. Yes to human magic. Set the stage and make hiring part of your brand's signature welcome. The first act of hospitality is in your hands.

HELP WANTED

> **REFLECTION PROMPTS**
>
> Here are three brainpokes to help you prepare for hosting a Super Skill interview.
>
> - Did your last interview seek truffles or mushrooms?
> - What rare, precious qualities do the team members who best embody your brand share?
> - How can you sharpen your instincts and attain mastery as a Super Skills tracker?

8
The Golden Rules Of Unorthodox Interviewing

Hiring is your first act of hospitality. You never need to be brash or rude. You are not just a hiring manager; you are a host, a story connector, a guardian of hospitality's storied heritage.

Etiquette guide for the human magic interviewer

While hiring approaches may modernise and hospitality may innovate, good etiquette – respectful conduct, listening with intent, and treating others with dignity – never goes out of style.

Minding your manners is minding your business. A dismissive tone, careless comments, or inconsistent process can cause irreversible damage both within and outside your business. Hiring is not just an administrative task; it is a branding opportunity.

Unorthodox interviewing does not mean abandoning structure or the rule of law. Instead, it focuses on developing a new framework. This involves crafting a process that embodies your values, amplifies your brand message, honours your candidates, and brings you closer to hiring your team of hospitality alchemists.

This is about reconnecting with the true purpose of hiring. That means rebuilding trust with a part of the business that you may have long side-eyed with annoyance and dismissed as unimportant.

Even magical societies abide by rules. The International Brotherhood of Magicians and the International Federation of Magic Societies (Fédération Internationale des Sociétés Magiques) have codes of ethics that guide members on matters of secrecy, performance conduct, and safeguarding the community's integrity (Roya, 2019). These golden rules honour magic as an art form and protect its sustainability for future generations.

Manners maketh magic

Let's picture your new approach in action. Some interviewers are content to muddle along, but not you. You are channelling the spirit of the arbiter of proper decorum, *Debrett's New Guide to Etiquette and Modern Manners* (Morgan, 1996), and informed by the timeless hiring principles from *People Resourcing* (Taylor, 2005), seasoned with the unwritten rules of stage magic.

Drawing on Taylor's list of thirteen problems with interviews and unprofessional interviewer behaviour, here are five enduring codes of conduct. Embracing these principles enables interviewers to uphold dignity, fairness, and discernment while offering protection against the adverse consequences of poor interviewing protocol.

Five golden etiquette rules

These rules may not be glamorous, but they are golden. They protect you and your business from missteps that can result in reputational damage and legal woes:

1. **Beware the self-fulfilling prophecy (aka the Nostradamus effect).** Do not ask questions only to validate your first impression. Stay open and curious.

2. **Watch for halo or horns.** Charm is not competence. A slow start does not mean a write-off. Suspend judgement. Remain curious. Be gracious.

3. **Avoid the 'personal liking' trap.** This is not a friend audition. Hire for impact, not chemistry with you. Trust and capacity to contribute matter more than social clique membership.

4. **Sidestep the 'just like me' bias.** Similarity does not equal suitability. Homogeneous hiring and copy-and-paste decisions limit resilience and healthy growth.

5. **Manage information overload.** Do not decide in five minutes. Listen deeply. Choose wisely.

The high price of getting it wrong

Poor etiquette not only leads to weak hires but also erodes trust, which can cause cultural decline, reputational damage, and PR crises. Hiring is hospitality, and hospitality is your brand in motion. Every interview is a moment of brand truth.

Perilous interviewer psychology

Interviewing is like driving. Most people believe they are above-average drivers, and many interviewers assume they are better than they are. The result? Overconfidence and speed are a dangerous combination.

This is a classic example of the Dunning–Kruger effect, a cognitive bias where individuals with limited knowledge or experience overestimate their abilities. At the same time, those with greater skill might undervalue themselves (Farnam Street, no date, a). In interviews this can lead to poorly structured questions, snap judgements, or misplaced confidence in gut feel over actual evidence.

There is more, though. Many hiring managers seldom receive honest, critical feedback on their interview techniques. Worse still, the consequences of poor interviews often do not become apparent immediately, sometimes not until months later, when that new hire proves to be misaligned, unproductive, or toxic to the team culture. Alternatively, this may occur if a candidate has a negative or unprofessional experience during the interview.

The root problem? Mistaking competence in one domain (eg finance, marketing, culinary) for interviewing mastery. Interviewing is a distinct and separate craft, and many are practising it with little evaluation, reflection, or accountability.

Let us be clear, there is no such thing as an expert interviewer. There are only those who are continually learning, refining, and practising.

Want to become a master interviewer? A candidate whisperer? Read on.

Trusting your intuition comes with a caveat

Contrary to conventional interviewing dogma, intuition is not the enemy. It can be a valuable asset if treated with care and respect.

In Human Magic Hiring, your instinctive impression of a candidate is not something to ignore. As an interviewer, your whole self – intellect, emotion, experience, and energy – is in the room. Your spirit may respond positively or hesitantly. That is natural. It is human.

However, here is the caveat: *You need to slow down!*

Treat intuition as a hypothesis, not a conclusion. Instead of rushing for confirmation, use the conversation to test your initial impression. Ask yourself:

- Is what I sensed unfolding in their story?
- Do their responses confirm or contradict that early signal?

Slow interviewing allows this to happen. The thoughtful pacing, the counterintuitive Super Skills questions, the pauses – all of these give you space to work backwards and either verify or disprove your initial assumptions.

When done well, intuitive judgement does not replace evidence; it enhances it. It sharpens your awareness but must always be followed by open-minded inquiry, not assumption, together with the willingness to be proved wrong.

Record your findings like an anthropologist

Ditch the tired interview assessment scorecards. When interviewing for Super Skills, you are a field researcher. A cultural botanist. A story-catcher.

Practise the art of *noticing*. Use fieldnotes to record detail and nuance. Capture body language, story arcs, tone shifts. Separate facts from feelings. Spot the threads of Super Skills and personal values.

Use this three-part method:

1. **Observe:** Facts, quotes, cues
2. **Interpret:** Patterns, themes, possible Super Skills
3. **Reflect:** Your internal response and energy

Let's unpack the details.

1. Observe: Facts, quotes, cues

Record what takes place:

- Date, time, location
- Interviewers present
- Standout quotes or phrases

- Physical cues – gestures, tone, posture
- Energy cues – laughter, warmth, hesitation

This is your descriptive layer – what Schwandt (2015) calls 'factual data […] settings, actions, behaviours'.

Remember to keep an open mind, not to make judgements.

2. Interpret: Patterns, themes, possible Super Skills

Now ask yourself:

- What Super Skills emerged, and how strong are they?
- What patterns or contradictions stood out?
- How might they contribute to creating hospitality alchemy with the team?

This is your *So what?* zone. Interpret with care and a judicious dash of imagination.

3. Reflect: Your internal response and energy

Be honest and accurate as you consider:

- What resonated or felt off?

- Did the interview flow make you feel energised or hesitant?
- Did the conversation shift your view?
- What surprised you?

Schwandt (2015) calls this *introspective commentary*. The focus here is on emotional awareness, not bias.

Remember that in most countries, fieldnotes – like any other recruitment records – might become legal evidence. The way you document interviews says as much about your professionalism as your policies do. Being meticulous leads to fewer regrets in hiring decisions.

When recorded consistently, fieldnotes reveal the DNA of your best hires. Over time patterns will emerge. You will spot your property's unique pattern of Super Skills – human magic qualities in team members who bring your hospitality values to life.

Interviewing is not about polish; it is about presence. Observe well, and the magic will reveal itself. With these golden rules in hand, you are ready to embrace the full Three-Course Conversation interview framework of appetiser, entrée, and dessert. Let's get started.

REFLECTION PROMPTS

- Refresh your memory about the five golden interview etiquette rules.
- Prepare your human magic interview fieldnote framework.
- What is one step you can take to showcase your brand's hospitality in your next interview?
- Are you ready to turn hiring into your brand's signature welcome?

9

How To Host Interviews Like A Hearty Supper Club Gathering

What if your next interview felt less like a high-stakes interrogation and more like a soul-nourishing supper club? Imagine a captivating gathering around a weathered oak table, filled with lively conversation, curiosity, and care.

Let's look at how to achieve this.

A step-by-step guide to supper club-style interviews

By following these seven steps, you can transform your interview style:

1. Lay down the welcome mat.

2. Ditch the desk, set the table.

3. Welcome your guest.

4. Prepare quality questions.

5. Serve the three-course conversation.

6. Savour the stories.

7. Remember the supper club setting.

Step one: Lay down the welcome mat

Model the care and attention you want your employees to lavish on your guests.

Forget the cold conference room. Avoid the noisy café. Close the laptop. Ask yourself, *How can I create a space where this person feels safe enough to be real?* As a thoughtful host, you set the tone. Remove distractions that distract you and disrupt the flow. Imagine instead a warm, generous, and deliberate space. Think of it as an intimate supper club atmosphere, with soft lighting, a leisurely pace, and even the sound of laughter. These are the signs of genuine connection you want. You are not conducting an interview; you are creating a humanity-affirming experience. Being radically present is a delightfully unexpected exception to the norm.

Hosting is a sacred act. Your candidate is your guest, and a seat at the table is reserved for them. Make them feel seen, heard, and genuinely welcomed. When people feel safe, they lower their guard and reveal who they truly are.

Calm their nerves. Take your time. You will be rewarded with doors opening to deeper insights into your candidate's character.

This is the heart of the supper club-inspired Three-Course Conversation interview.

Step two: Ditch the desk, set the table

Unorthodox interviewers prepare thoughtfully, set the tone with intention, and invite connection.

Do your mental mise en place. Ground yourself. Prepare to uncover values, beliefs, and those hard-to-fake human Super Skills. You do not need another internet-sourced list of standard questions. You need a fresh framework to connect with people on a level that speaks to their capacity for human magic.

Used well, this approach helps you build a team of hospitality alchemists. You are looking for individuals who blend technical competence, Super Skills, and emotional depth to craft unforgettable experiences.

Step Three: Welcome your guest

Like a skilled maître d', you oversee the candidate's interview experience from start to finish. From seating arrangements to timing, you guide the flow with a confident yet gentle touch. Your presence matters, and your energy is contagious. Greet your candidate warmly, just as you would a cherished guest at your table.

You are the glue that holds experience and process together. Create a calm, open atmosphere. When people feel truly welcomed, they relax, and that relaxation becomes the pathway to richer stories, deeper insights, and more authentic connection.

Step Four: Prepare quality questions

Competency interviews skim the surface. You are here to uncover personality, spirit, and the spark of Super Skills. As noted in the FS blog, 'The quality of the answers we get is directly correlated with the quality of the questions we ask' (Farnam Street, no date, b).

You are listening for the ten Super Skills – the ones that seldom appear on CVs and LinkedIn profiles. You are chasing stories, not just curated summaries. Like a master sommelier, you select Super Skill questions that will best complement your candidate's personality in each course. You pair and serve these questions to enhance the conversation flow and reveal the actual person behind the candidate profile.

When receiving your candidate's responses, ask yourself:

- What shaped this person?
- What lights them up?
- What will lead them closer to doing more of what they love?

Adam Mastroianni puts it perfectly: 'Good conversations have lots of doorknobs' – easy ways to enter and exit, many places to grab onto and go somewhere else Mastroianni (2022).

Turn your questions into doorknobs by creating easy, natural entry points that invite deeper dialogue. Pay close attention to the doorknobs your candidate leans towards. These questions and responses reveal passions, reflect lived values, or unlock a key insight. Follow where the candidate leads; that is where the treasure lies.

Step Five: Serve the three-course conversation

Inspired by the unrushed rhythm of a supper club, this conversational-style interview menu unfolds like a memorable meal, shown here with serving time guidelines:

- **Appetiser.** Light, intriguing openers. Amuse-bouche questions to invite connection.

> Allow fifteen minutes for this course to warm up the atmosphere.

- **Entrée.** Deep storytelling and discovery. The hearty middle course, where personal values and Super Skills surface, and you take note of them. Allow sixty minutes for the entrée to be served and savoured.

- **Dessert.** Reflective, aspirational prompts tie hopes, dreams, and meaning for both the candidate and your business. Allow thirty minutes for this course, to sweeten to taste.

This is a story-sharing framework that provides space for natural conversational flow while being rooted in a structure that enables the candidate's unique human qualities to shine.

Step Six: Savour the stories

Slow things down – this is not fast-food hiring. This is a hearty, home-cooked process, prepared with care, seasoned with curiosity, and warmed by respect. Great interviews are like great meals – shared, savoured, and remembered. When you leave room for real stories, you find resilience born of loss, creativity under constraint, courage shaped by uncertainty, and curiosity sparked by play. Each story shared is a window into personal values, Super Skills, and hidden genius.

These are the flavour notes of human magic. Make time to savour them.

Step Seven: Remember the supper club setting

The conversational-style interview approach is not about being nice. It is about being intentional. If you treat interviews like one-way interrogations, you lose not only candidates but also opportunities.

Super Skill interviewing is another way to create value for your candidate through unexpected, memorable career conversations. It is an opportunity to cultivate goodwill towards your brand from candidates you do not select to join your team as well as from those you do hire. When hiring for human magic, you are simultaneously celebrating your candidate's individuality and determining their unique contribution to the collective, whether that is to your existing team or the new one you are assembling.

Interviewing successfully for human magic requires discipline, intuition, and care. It is not HR fluff; it is foundational to your business success.

In the next chapter your curated pantry of powerful questions will be matched to the ten Super Skills.

HELP WANTED

Take your seat. Adjust your napkin. Let us explore how to serve each course with insight, attention, and a dash of magic.

> **REFLECTION PROMPTS**
> - How can you create a welcoming space that will invite authenticity from your candidates?
> - What elements of human magic are you most hoping to uncover?
> - What questions will be most likely to reveal meaningful stories and the candidates' Super Skills?

PART THREE
THE HOW

10
Appetiser – Starting With Amuse-Bouche Questions

First impressions matter. Human magic often unfolds in the opening moments, when you invite someone into an unexpected conversation and they are instantly captivated. That is when the dance begins.

As the host, your job is to stir intrigue and offer comfort. Lead with warmth, surprise, and a touch of delight. Welcome your candidate as a guest, and begin by serving an amuse-bouche.

An amuse-bouche – a 'mouth delighter' – is a tiny, imaginative morsel designed to whet the appetite, stir the senses, and rouse the imagination. It is not on the menu; it arrives as a surprise, and its purpose is to charm. In the interview, an amuse-bouche question works the same way: it's small, playful, and unexpected. Its role is to disarm your candidate, coax them into story-sharing, and signal that this will not be a conventional interview.

The power of an amuse-bouche question

Before delving into the more substantial appetiser course questions, ask a playful opener to warm up the confident conversationalist or gently encourage the quiet candidate.

I once asked a nervous candidate which cooking smell made them feel comforted and transported them to a special place. For a whole minute, their eyes brimmed with emotion, their entire face lighting up. They then shared a story rich in emotion and sprinkled with Super Skills. That is the power of the amuse-bouche question.

Serve your appetiser questions

Once you've broken the ice, it's time to move on to the appetiser questions. In a restaurant, amuse-bouches are off-menu surprises from the chef, while appetisers are the dishes chosen to start the meal. In an interview, appetiser questions are more substantial than the playful openers, but not as much as the main course. They are designed to stimulate appetite and interest to engage in deeper conversation – questions

APPETISER – STARTING WITH AMUSE-BOUCHE QUESTIONS

that gently explore values, motivation, and the stories behind someone's human magic.

Appetiser questions are not your typical fare. Candidates may be taken aback, even stunned into momentary silence. That is absolutely fine. Resist the urge to fill the space. This is where silence often plays its part. If your candidate pauses, remain calm. That stillness might be the moment when truth and memory meet. Breathe. Offer a nod. Let the silence linger. Offer kind eyes instead of quick commentary. Perhaps your candidate's brilliance needs a gentler pace and you to create a trusting space.

Ask yourself: *What insight is being stirred here? What sits behind their hesitation?*

You are not just gathering answers; you are uncovering the person behind the polish – the values, quirks, trials, and quiet strengths that could make them a remarkable hire.

Let your patience make room for reflection, and genuine stories start to flow. Light questions that open the conversation often reveal the interesting stories. You want to find out:

- What makes them tick
- What motivates them to grow
- What makes their human magic shimmer

Pay attention: subtle cues in how your candidate responds will reveal character insights and indicate how they might respond to guests, teammates, and the unpredictable rhythms of service.

BOLO and Red Flag alerts

Be on the lookout for early signals of Super Skills sparks, substance, and energy alignment.

BOLO: Look for...	Red Flag: Watch out for...
Spark that can't be faked – a visible lift in tone, posture, or pace when conversation topics matter to them	Flatline – no energy shift, rehearsed lines, rote answers, or a monotone voice mask
Comfort in silence – they sit in the pause, breathe, reflect, then respond thoughtfully	Fills or flees – can't sit with silence; rushes filler, freezes, or deflects under pause
Stories you can see and feel – vivid, specific examples with clear roles, actions, and outcomes, ownership described	Foggy tales – vague generalities, waffling without specifics, 'we' without 'I', or gaps in what's unsaid
Values in action – decisions and behaviours that reflect authenticity and what they claim to value	Values in words only – fine words, but examples reveal ego excess, convenience, or transactional thinking
Words and body language in sync – posture, tone, and story all light up together	Mismatch – stories shared are at odds with body language

APPETISER – STARTING WITH AMUSE-BOUCHE QUESTIONS

Don't spend the appetiser course on small talk alone. This is where you look for the first signs of Super Skills: spark, substance, and sincerity. You are not looking for perfection. You are looking for their presence and the distinctive qualities of their character. Remember, the smallest questions, asked with curiosity and care, can reveal the richest seams of human magic.

Pay equal attention to pauses and body language as to what's said. This is how you will begin to recognise the genuine person beneath the polish, and whether their human magic belongs at your table.

This is not a performance test. It is a puzzle – a delicious one.

Amuse-bouche and appetiser questions

Here is a brief list of examples to give you inspiration for the questions that will work best with your candidates.

 Sample interview questions

Imagine you are hosting a dream supper club:

- Who is gathered around your table (eight guests, living or dead)?
- Why these people?
- How would they get along?

What are the top three songs on your favourite playlist?

- What does this playlist say about you?
- What memories or moods do these tracks evoke?

What book, or article, recently shook and changed how you see the world? (Interviewer note: Swap in eg film, video, or podcast interview if better for your candidate.)

- How did it shake you?
- Did it lead you to change your mindset or behaviour?

What is your greatest superpower or genius?

- What do you do that feels effortless but amazes others?

What is your kryptonite?

- What drains you or leaves you uninspired?

This is not a script to follow line by line. These are questions designed to elicit a laugh, a pause, a sparkle of self-discovery. They give your candidate the chance to surprise even themselves.

Use one as an amuse-bouche. Two or more as appetisers. Pair them. Freestyle. Let curiosity be your guide.

Take field notes – verbal answers, seemingly inconsequential titbits from a casual comment, body language, energy shifts. These small details often reveal the most significant truths.

APPETISER – STARTING WITH AMUSE-BOUCHE QUESTIONS

Your next course is the entrée. In it you will explore and uncover your candidate's character notes and the Super Skill strengths of your next culture shaper.

> **REFLECTION PROMPTS**
> - What opening questions have you naturally used in the past?
> - What new amuse-bouche and appetiser questions would work well in the next interview you'll host?
> - How will you adjust your opening approach in your next candidate interview?

11
Entrée: Revealing Your Candidate's Super Skills Combo

Tired of mis-hires, culture mismatches, and conversations that lead nowhere? If past interviews have left you with a sour taste, this main course corrects that.

After the appetiser warms up your candidate, the entrée is where you serve the substance It is designed as a deliberate transition from snapshots to tangible evidence gathering. This is the course where character is revealed, human magic simmers to the surface, and stories unveil the Super Skills that make your candidate truly unforgettable.

Why the entrée is crucial

The term entrée, from the French *entrer* ('to enter'), marks the main event in fine dining. In your Human Magic Hiring approach, it is the meaty middle – the hearty exchange where values, beliefs, and experiences surface with flavour.

This course offers more than answers. It invites complexity and narrative richness – the sort of depth that reveals how an individual will show up, serve others, and help shape your culture. Do not skip the entrée. Your next culture shaper may be hiding just beneath a surface-level answer, and this is your moment to go deeper.

A reminder of the ten Super Skills

These enduring qualities are essential flavour notes of your candidate's unique human magic and the foundational ingredients crucial for hospitality alchemy:

1. **Empathy** – intuitively sensing and responding meaningfully to others

2. **Kindness** – radiating genuine warmth and thoughtful care

3. **Curiosity** – enjoying an exploratory, questioning mindset

4. **Creativity** – improvising and solving problems imaginatively

5. **Unlearn learning** – letting go of the obsolete and embracing the new

6. **Gratitude** – expressing appreciation with meaning and generosity

7. **Vulnerability** – being open and authentic

8. **Courage** – boldly acting beyond conventional thinking and the status quo

9. **Resilience** – maintaining grace under pressure, with the ability to bounce back and bounce forwards

10. **Purpose connection** – aligning personal values and motivation with the organisation's vision and mission

Hosting the conversation and steering the flow

When interviewing for Super Skills, think communal table rather than conference room to set the scene. Maintain the mood you created during the appetiser course: warm, unhurried, and rooted in attentive listening. Your goal, especially here in the entrée course, is to uncover the *understory* – the often-unspoken motivations, values, and perspectives that shape your candidate's actions and aspirations.

Ask thoughtful questions. Then give space for the answers to breathe.

Remember:

- Your candidate is the hero.
- You are the host, guide, and stage manager.
- Your conversations open the door to their inner world and their unique blend of Super Skills.
- This course is where you uncover who they really are.

Serve your entrée questions

For the best entrée course experience, select at least one question under each Super Skill. Time permitting, explore more – especially if the conversation is flowing and the candidate is sharing rich evidence of their skills in action. Use the BOLO alerts for each Super Skill to help you listen for clues in their stories.

Each candidate has a unique Super Skills profile. These gems often reveal themselves in tales of setbacks, triumphs, and good fortune. Your role is to give those stories room to unfold with a light guiding touch, not a controlling grip.

ENTRÉE: REVEALING YOUR CANDIDATE'S SUPER SKILLS COMBO

BOLO and Red Flag alerts

Be on the look out for the clues and cues in conversation that reveal whether Super Skills are lived realities or polished lines.

BOLO: Look for...	Red Flag: Watch out for...
Stories with substance – rich, specific examples that reveal lived experience	Polished but hollow – rehearsed or borrowed generic answers with no real detail
Values in action – alignment between what they believe and say, and how they've behaved	Values mismatch – stated beliefs and principles that don't show up in their stories
Natural brilliance – flashes of 'knack-fors' (tacit knowledge), Super Skills that training can't teach – eg empathy, creativity, or resilience	Skill by script – reliance on jargon or textbook language, no spark of natural brilliance or innate talents in their stories
Energy and engagement – enthusiasm and vitality when talking about challenges and successes	Flat energy – detached tone, little passion or connection to their own experiences
Curve balls and contradictions – surprising details or tensions that reveal depth and nuance	Avoidance or deflection – vague answers, subject changes, or reluctance to dig into the conversation

The entrée course gives your candidate the opportunity to reveal their distinctive Super Skills. Your job is to follow the breadcrumbs: take note of their natural brilliance, the alignment between their words and actions, and the stories that hint at deeper truths. One thoughtful entrée question, asked with curiosity and care, can uncover more than a dozen rushed ones.

Entrée questions

Mix up your questioning. Closed questions, often requiring a simple 'yes' or 'no', can break the ice, provide clarity, and bring the conversation back on track – eg 'Are you happy in your current role?'

Open questions invite depth and are a gateway to further discovery – eg 'When did you last feel proud of your contribution at work?' Together, they create balance: structure without stifling, freedom without drift.

Channel your inner sleuth by asking yourself *Do their stories ring true?* And *How can I tease truths, tests, and triumphs from the conversation thread?*

These examples are designed to help you cultivate a list of clarifying questions best suited to bringing your candidate's understory out into the light during your next entrée interview.

 Sample clarifying questions
- Why did you do that?
- What surprised you?

ENTRÉE: REVEALING YOUR CANDIDATE'S SUPER SKILLS COMBO

- How did you feel?
- What would you do differently next time?
- How will you apply what you learned?

These are not trick questions. Instead, they aim to reveal genuine stories and emotions, acting as bridge questions for deeper understanding and connection.

Keep your field notes focused

Take observational notes on verbal answers, seemingly inconsequential titbits from a casual comment, body language, energy shifts. Focus also on:

- What they said
- Which Super Skills surfaced
- How their story made you feel
- What deeper meaning you glimpsed

The more tuned-in and specific your notes, the more clearly you will recognise whether this candidate brings the Super Skills combination your team needs.

Save room for dessert, the grand finale. End on a sweet note by uncovering any last Super Skill nuggets and sealing the impression you want to leave. Make your candidate feel seen, valued, and hosted, because how you close the interview is how they'll remember your brand.

> **REFLECTION PROMPTS**
> - What questions have you used in the main sections of previous interviews? How effective were they?
> - What new entrée questions would work well in helping you uncover candidates' Super Skills?
> - What one change can you make to ensure your Super Skills interview closes with human magic, not just standard procedure?

12
Dessert – Wrapping Up With Intention

First impressions matter. What about final impressions, though? They endure. The interview is not over until dessert is served. It's time now to finish the interview with a sweet, refined flourish. This is not a standard interview wrap-up with rushed formalities. It is an alchemical moment.

The word dessert originates from the fourteenth-century French term *desservir*, meaning 'to clear the table'.

Fittingly, this course clears misconceptions, questions earlier assumptions, and reveals truths that leave a lasting impression. It signals final decisions and sets the tone for what follows.

Dessert is more than a sweet ending. In hospitality, it is the grand finale where chefs showcase their artistry. Meanwhile, hosts linger longer, ensuring their guests feel seen, cared for, and delighted.

Continue hosting your candidate with care and intention, as there may well still be a few final golden nuggets to uncover. Like prized truffles, Super Skills lie buried deep within virtues, flaws, passions, and pains. They are only revealed when the interviewer creates an atmosphere of safety and trust, and the candidate believes that atmosphere to be genuine.

As the dessert course draws to a close, do not miss the chance to serve those last sweet notes of care and connection. Imagine how your candidate feels when they finish an interview where not just their job-related skills but their full humanity is welcomed, where they do not feel the pressure to edit their story or mute parts of their personality to fit in.

Human magic in interviewing never ends with abrupt, formal stiffness. Craft a warm, attentive, memorable, and distinctive finale that reflects the true spirit of your brand and your personality. This is where you sign off with your signature of authentic hospitality in hiring.

Remember, as an unorthodox interviewer, you are hosting your candidate at a table where their personality quirks and their unique Super Skills combination are celebrated, even if they are not the perfect match for your organisation's culture.

DESSERT – WRAPPING UP WITH INTENTION

Don't rush this course. Skipping the chance to savour the final moments leaves a sour aftertaste. It breaks the trust built in the appetiser course and undoes the connection made during the entrée. You end by closing doors instead of opening them.

The importance of the dessert course

In a world obsessed with speed, those who slow down stand out. By accentuating the dessert course, you enjoy the full luxury and decadence of slow interviewing.

Stay present. Let the emails and operational demands wait. During dessert, a relaxed candidate will reveal yet more clues about their Super Skill capacity, values, and aspirations. Your presence maintains the magic.

The dessert course is the final part of your Three-Course Conversation interview. It is where you:

- Bring the candidate's story full circle
- Thank them sincerely for their time and openness
- Determine if their human magic adds a meaningful note to your culture
- Envision how their Super Skills complement your existing team's flavour profile

- Find out if this is the character you need to write your next brand chapter

A well-executed dessert course:

- Increases chances of hiring a culture-amplifier alchemist, not just a culture fit
- Gives candidates a lived experience of the hospitality you expect your team to deliver
- Demonstrates brand synergy and alignment between the guest and employee experiences
- Builds trust and goodwill, even among those you do not hire
- Enhances employer brand and long-term employee loyalty and advocacy
- Reinforces belief in your leadership and values

Your job adverts do not define your employer brand. It is the story candidates and employees share about how you made them feel that does, which makes this final impression so important. Do they leave uplifted, or diminished? Does your hiring process make them feel distinguished or disenfranchised? Fail to connect genuinely, and you invite misunderstanding and reputational risk.

Even more damaging is when your internal culture clashes with your external narrative, which equates to

DESSERT – WRAPPING UP WITH INTENTION

a betrayal of your brand values and promise. People notice and talk about this and spread the bad news.

Unorthodox interviewers are not impressed by polish. They are moved by depth. They are drawn to candidates who offer a unique story, not just a bland or borrowed script. This final course is your chance to honour the whole person before you. Let them leave not just having been interviewed but feeling truly seen.

Imagine the power of being hired for who you are, where your story, your strengths, your magic are valued so they can be developed for mutual benefit, not exploited. When delivered with integrity and care, the dessert course becomes the ultimate act of hospitality, crafting a finale so memorable, it becomes its own story.

BOLO and Red Flag alerts

Be on the lookout for sweet harmony: authenticity, energy, and human depth.

BOLO: Look for...	Red Flag: Watch out for...
A heart for hospitality – a natural hosting mindset that feels genuine	No feel for hospitality – answers lack warmth or service instinct
Clarity about your brand – understanding of your culture, purpose, values, and mission	Vague grasp of your brand – generic and superficial responses that could apply anywhere

BOLO: Look for...	Red Flag: Watch out for...
Thoughtful contribution – clear reflections on how they can add value and make an impact	Unclear direction – little sense of motivation or personal impact
Strong self-awareness and values – integrity, confidence, grounded self-worth	Weak articulation – struggles to express personal strengths or unique value
Curiosity with care – questions that show interest in people and growth, not just ambition	Superficial engagement – flat, evasive, or over-polished answers; rushed or transactional

The dessert course is about clarity and connection. These final conversations reveal alignment and the unique blend of care and Super Skills a candidate brings. Listen for both sweet notes and sour ones. With curiosity and discernment, you'll spot the candidates whose human magic will leave a lasting impression and who are ideally suited to your hospitality brand.

> **Pro interviewer tip**
>
> Think like a sommelier making that final wine pairing.
>
> You are a story connector. Will this candidate bring harmony, distinction, and nuance to your team, or tension?

Questions for the dessert course

Use dessert questions to close strong. Uncover the final Super Skills and leave your candidate with the lingering flavour of your hospitality brand long after the interview ends. Here are just a few examples of questions to help end with flourish and finesse.

(?) Inviting personal reflection

- If your personality were a dessert dish, what would it be, and why?

(?) Turning the tables

- What is one question you wish I had asked you? Why is it important to you? (Note: Be ready to answer the question they put to you.)
- What questions would you like to ask me?

(?) Welcoming feedback

- What three words describe your experience of this interview? Sweet notes? Sour notes?
- What should we keep, stop, or start?

(?) Gauging compatibility

- Describe the kind of team culture in which you flourish.

Determining aspirations
- What is one bold goal or dream you are quietly nurturing?
- How would joining our team help move that dream forward?

 Valuing personality and reciprocity
- In a nutshell, what makes you and your story unforgettable?
- How will you honour that story here?
- What do you need from us to make that possible?

An important point to remember throughout this course is that Super Skills by themselves are non-moral. According to the dictionary definition in Merriam-Webster (Merriam-Webster, no date), they are not classified as related to morality or ethics; neither moral nor immoral, neither good nor bad. It is how an individual chooses to utilise their Super Skills that determines whether the effect is positive or negative. Always keep this in mind when hiring for human magic. To assist you, each Super Skill discussed in Part Four includes a section that describes its potential shadow side.

Are you ready to tuck in?

Let us move on to where all meaningful hospitality begins – with Super Skills.

DESSERT – WRAPPING UP WITH INTENTION

REFLECTION PROMPTS

- How have you wrapped interviews up in the past?
- What new dessert questions will give you the perfect finale to your next interview?
- What signals will tell you that your candidate felt seen, valued, and well hosted in the finale, the dessert course?

PART FOUR
THE SUPER SKILLS

13
Super Skill 1: Empathy

Empathy is the cornerstone of care, transforming ordinary interactions into extraordinary human connections.

Empathy is the ability to intuitively sense and respond to others' feelings without prejudging. It requires us to recognise and share in the thoughts and emotions of others – to see things from their point of view.

With empathy as a core element of hospitality, guest experiences feel natural, intuitive, effortless, and memorable. At the heart of authentic hospitality, you will find a team that is bustling with care, understanding, generosity, and insight.

The power of empathy

Often dismissed as weak or soft, empathy is the underdog Super Skill with a quiet bark but a powerful bite. It is the master key that unlocks the door to multiple Super Skills and opportunities to create human magic. Without empathy, no kindness, unlearn learning, creativity, or real connection exists. Without it, there can be no cohesive team, emotional intelligence, unforgettable experiences, or hospitality alchemy.

Manifesting empathy is like wearing a pair of X-ray glasses to see emotions in high definition. You can see and appreciate the world from another person's perspective while remaining conscious of your emotional blind spots and biases. As a fully developed Super Skill, empathy involves accepting differences, which can be uncomfortable and challenging. As Brené Brown explains (Brown, 2021), empathy is not simply about walking in someone else's shoes; it's about listening with belief and trust to what an experience is like for the other person, even when it would be very different for you.

Individuals who demonstrate a high level of empathy tend to show openness, curiosity, consideration, and discernment. They are masters of finding common ground, even in the trickiest interactions.

Crucially, empathy flourishes when backed by clear and compassionate boundaries. Emotionally intelligent individuals avoid sacrificing their wellbeing on the altar of service delivery. There is no glory in being a burnout martyr, regardless of the cause. They recognise when to ask for help, how to accept support, and how to safeguard their energy.

Understanding the relationship between empathy and other human qualities is vital. According to Brown (2021), empathy is a powerful tool within compassion and daily practice, rooted in recognising shared humanity rather than superiority. Brené Brown reminds us that genuine compassion never says, *I can fix you*. It says, *I'm with you*. Brown insists that empathy must not be mistaken for sympathy. While empathy connects people by conveying a sense of 'me too', sympathy often keeps emotional distance with the message of 'not me'.

Empathy is not just a response to suffering such as service failures or communication missteps. It can also amplify joy. When empathy is both reactive and proactive, guiding actions to uplift others, we enter the realm of positive empathy.

According to Morelli, Lieberman, and Zaki (2015), positive empathy occurs when individuals are motivated to uplift another person's positive emotion and subsequently vicariously experience a positive emotional state from taking that action. It plays a central role in building healthy community relationships, influencing team behaviour, and creating truly generous, one-of-a-kind hospitality.

Caution: The shadow side of empathy

Warm-glow empathy is connection-oriented, but it can lack depth, nuance, or genuine reciprocity. In hospitality, this might appear as superficial friendliness without follow-through or as grand gestures that centre on the server or host more than the guest.

Brown states in *Atlas of the Heart* (2021) that empathy in practice has two main components:

1. **Cognitive empathy:** The ability to recognise and intellectually understand another person's emotions
2. **Affective empathy:** The ability to emotionally resonate with and feel another's experience

Meaningful human connection, whether guest-facing or behind the scenes, requires both types of empathy.

When misused or left unchecked, empathy can also lead to emotional exhaustion, blurred boundaries, and unproductive work relationships. In *Radical Candor* (Scott, 2017), Kim Scott introduces the concept of Ruinous Empathy® – when someone cares personally but avoids honesty or challenge. The result? Confusion, inaction, and unintended harm.

Examples of ruinous empathy include:

- Vague praise that stalls development
- Sugar-coated criticism that avoids real accountability
- Failing to speak up out of fear of embarrassment, creating longer-term consequences

Add to that the 'warm-glow effect' (Morelli, Lieberman, and Zaki, 2015). When empathy is used for self-congratulation rather than genuine support, it becomes clear why healthy boundaries and reflective motivation are vital to authentic empathy and a supportive, hospitality-focused culture.

The business case for empathy

In authentic hospitality, where many organisations drop the ball with their guests, empathy is your most valuable player. It forms the foundation for meaningful service correction and recovery in exceptional guest experiences. It feeds team harmony and a healthy work culture, which is crucial for delivering your company's brand promise. When you hire for empathy, you are not just filling a role but also creating a springboard for the other nine key Super Skills – an environment where human magic can flourish in every team interaction and guest experience.

Why empathy matters – impact snapshot

Empathy's influence is far-reaching. It is a vital ingredient in the secret recipe that makes your brand's appeal and emotional connection, including in:

- **Guest experience impact:** Empathy creates trust, emotional connection, and personalised experiences.
- **Team culture impact:** Empathy promotes psychological safety, minimises drama, and enhances collaboration.
- **Business impact:** Empathy enhances service recovery, guest and employee care, loyalty, and reputation as a human-led business.

BOLO ALERT

Signs of genuine empathy:

- Ability to read the mood and the moment, not just who is in the room
- Recognition of unspoken emotional cues and ability to respond accordingly
- Emotionally intelligent decisions beyond SOPs
- Aptitude to uplift others without diminishing or patronising them
- Proficiency in handling rudeness or tension with grace and fitting boundaries

- Appropriate humour, humility, and sincere remorse when handling connection misunderstandings and interpersonal errors
- Affinity for valuing and embracing differences as pathways to deeper understanding and connection

Signs of performative or misused empathy:

- Emotional detachment, disguised as professionalism
- Indifference towards others' experiences and perspectives
- Deflection of blame or responsibility when thoughts, decisions, and actions are examined
- Surface-level niceness and lack of meaningful follow-through
- Weak boundaries, over-identifying with others' emotions to the detriment of self, team, and the operation
- Display of warm-glow behaviour, with empathy used to feel good about themselves rather than uplift others

---

Pro interviewer tip

In the interview, delve deeper by probing for emotional accountability and self-awareness.

For example:

Is the approach win-lose- or win-win-focused?

How do they recharge and protect themselves from empathy fatigue?

Questions to uncover empathy

Here are just a few examples of questions for you to build on, to enable you to determine your candidate's capacity for empathy.

 Exploring understanding

- What is empathy? (Interview tip: Expect a confident simple definition. Probe deeper for insight and lived experience.)

 Understanding lived experience

Tell me about a time when someone special visited your home.

- What did you do to make them feel welcome?
- How did you know they were having a wonderful time?
- What would you do differently next time?

 Discussing personal appreciation

- How did someone show empathy to you recently?
- Can you think of an example from an expected source?

 Gauging emotional awareness

Imagine a guest or colleague appears upset but is not saying much.

- What subtle cues would you look for to understand how they are genuinely feeling?
- Share a specific situation where you adapted your interaction approach based on what you observed rather than what the other person said.

❓ Discovering personal stories

Describe a situation where someone confided in you about their struggles or challenges that you personally found difficult to relate to.

- How did you respond?
- What did you learn from that experience?

14
Super Skill 2: Kindness

Genuine kindness is a subtle yet mighty force that reminds us of our shared humanity. Acts of kindness shape memorable hospitality experiences for both guests and team members.

Kindness involves thinking and acting with empathy and compassion. It springs from sincere concern for another's wellbeing, opinions, and experiences. Kindness can take the form of bold actions or discreet gestures, with both being equally impactful.

The initial steps can start with small, generous gestures that lift the mood – holding a door open, offering a word of encouragement, sharing a smile, or delivering a cup of tea unasked, exactly when it is most needed. However, because its impact is subtly profound, kindness often remains underrated despite its significant positive influence, and like empathy, it is frequently misunderstood as 'soft'.

The power of kindness

A kind gesture can turn a negative experience into a positive one, and a listening ear can offer hope where there is despair.

Authentic acts of kindness are never performative or self-serving. Genuine acts of kindness, supported by courage and conviction, have a cumulative effect as an antidote to negative behaviours such as meanness, apathy, selfishness, or rudeness, which, if left unchecked, can be disastrous to your company's culture.

Imagine a workplace where kindness is an active, regenerative force. Lois Blyth refers to it as, 'habitual kindness; hard to give kindness; being kind before you have received kindness; being kind because it is simply the right thing to do; being kind even if you have a sense of dislike for someone; loving kindness and forgiving kindness' (Blyth, 2015).

Whether random or deliberate, selfless, or reciprocal, kindness is the super glue that holds human connections together. It brings us together in a kind-hearted bond; when we are kind to one another, energy shifts and a kind of contagious alchemy flows.

Caution: The shadow side of kindness

Kindness can be misused when motivated by a preoccupation with image, insecurity, or a desire to avoid conflict. When kindness is used as a virtue-signalling tool or for self-promotion, its genuine effect is diminished and legitimate connections are eroded.

When assembling a team for hospitality, it is valuable to conduct a brief audit of an individual's acts of kindness as part of a team health check. Consider: Are their actions genuinely motivated by care and compassion, or are they more about seeking praise, prestige, or career advancement?

In *The Little Pocket Book of Kindness* (Blyth, 2015), Lois Blyth issues a sharp warning to beware of the enemies of kindness – cynicism, doubt, suspicion, self-interest, and selfishness. Left unchecked in the workplace, these attitudes corrode cultures, making kindness seem naïve and even weak. What follows? Minimal effort, apathy, blame games, and fractured trust.

Similar to the damaging effects of Ruinous Empathy® (Scott, 2017) mentioned in the previous chapter, kindness without boundaries turns into people pleasing. In these situations, individuals may allow others to take advantage of them, tolerate unacceptable behaviour, and avoid necessary confrontation. Kindness then becomes a shield that deflects accountability. For example, a team member may avoid speaking out to spare feelings, only to watch the entire team suffer from performance issues that team member was too 'kind' to address.

The business case for kindness

Kindness is an active agent in creating a healthy, vibrant culture. Like yeast in bread, kindness acts as a leavening agent that helps your team rise to the challenge of delivering extraordinary experiences and memorable moments. It nurtures team trust, deepens guest relationships, and strengthens community ties.

Psychologist Claudia Hammond, summarising a major kindness study led by Prof. Robin Banerjee at the University of Sussex, reframes kindness as reciprocal (Hammond, 2023). Even when it involves personal effort or discomfort, people are motivated to be kind, hoping that kindness will be returned when they need it most.

Organisational psychologist Adam Grant, in *Give and Take*, classifies professionals in terms of a reciprocity framework of takers, givers, and matchers (Grant, 2013).

- **Takers:** Self-focused, they take more than they give. They believe that the world is competitive and that to succeed, they must outdo others.
- **Givers:** Others-focused, they give more than they get. They prioritise other people's interests.

- **Matchers:** They give as much as they take and take as much as they give.

Typically, givers are plentiful in real life but thankfully rare in the workplace. Givers with a healthy touch of a matcher's discernment are the people you want on your hospitality alchemists team.

Why kindness matters – impact snapshot

Kindness is an intentional, daily, heart-led act. When you hire for kindness, you welcome a quiet force and an active agent to your team. Someone who will bring warmth, compassion, care, and thoughtful action to every guest interaction, team connection, and community engagement. No quid pro quo or strings attached.

- **Guest experience impact:** Kindness builds credible trust, emotional connection, and active care.

- **Team culture impact:** Kindness encourages mutual respect, dignity, and informal support systems, and a safe space to show vulnerability, experiment, learn from mistakes.

- **Business impact:** Kindness boosts morale and fosters brand engagement. It counteracts toxic cultures and emotionally stagnant systems.

BOLO ALERT

Signs of authentic kindness:

- Concrete examples of both selfless and reciprocal acts of kindness
- Personal stories of thoughtful responses that reflect care, pride, or joy in helping
- Evidence of subtle or bold, random, or intentional action (all types are equally valid)
- Appropriate sensitivity and discretion to a recipient's dignity, agency, and pride
- Willingness to receive kindness, especially during personal vulnerability or in difficult circumstances

Signs of performative or faux kindness:

- Kindness stories that are vague, insincere, and short on specific action taken
- Tonal intent that is 'off', with a whiff of virtue-signalling or a self-congratulatory tone
- Difficulties in recalling a recent time they received an act of kindness, indicating a lack of reciprocity
- Stories of kindness are misaligned with behavioural examples and non-verbal cues
- Motivations rooted in people pleasing or conflict avoidance
- Kindness used as a lever for their benefit or advantage (which is a taker warning)

SUPER SKILL 2: KINDNESS

> **Pro interviewer tip**
>
> Watch for signs of alignment between what they say and do. For instance, a candidate who tells a story about kindness but then rolls their eyes when mentioning a 'difficult' guest or colleague might indicate a disconnect between their stated value of kindness and their actual behaviour.
>
> Leave no assumption unchallenged. Probe further.

Questions to uncover kindness

Here are just a few examples of questions for you to build on, to enable you to determine your candidate's capacity for kindness.

 Exploring understanding

- What is kindness? (Interview tip: Anticipate a definition. Probe for a personal, lived understanding.)

 Determining the capacity for self-kindness

- How do you show kindness to yourself?

 Gauging reciprocity

- What is a memorable, random act of kindness you received?

169

- What was the situation?
- How did it make you feel?

 Discovering personal stories

Tell me about how you have supported someone who was facing difficulties but preferred to keep it private.

- How did you approach them?
- Why did you do it?
- How did it make you feel?
- How was your kindness received?
- Were you being as kind as you could be, or as kind as you needed to be?

 Considering any reluctance

- What makes you hesitant to help others?
- Does your hesitation change depending on the nature of your relationship with the person? (Interviewer note: Probing pointers could be family, colleague, acquaintance, someone in authority, someone they want to impress.)

15
Super Skill 3: Curiosity

Curicsity ignites inquiry, discovery, and transformative thinking, driving creativity and regenerative growth.

Curiosity reflects a mindset of wonder about other places and people. When activated, curiosity encourages people to explore different perspectives, discover new ideas, and gain deeper insights. It also fires up other Super Skills such as empathy, unlearn learning, and creativity.

In *Big Magic* (Gilbert, 2015), Elizabeth Gilbert tells us that 'Following that scavenger hunt of curiosity can lead you to amazing, unexpected places. […] Or it may lead you nowhere.'

The power of curiosity

Curiosity jumpstarts the pursuit of clues, prompting relentless questioning: *Why? Why not? What if?* That paves the way for unlearning what no longer serves a purpose, and also for embracing new knowledge that fuels creativity, experimentation, and transformative change.

Curiosity is more than having an interest or fleeting fascinations. Brené Brown explains in *Atlas of the Heart* (Brown, 2021) that interest is a cognitive openness to engaging with a topic. In contrast, curiosity involves a more profound emotional and cognitive pursuit of understanding. Harnessing your curiosity advantage requires vulnerability and courage to accept the reality that you do not have all the answers. It also requires a willingness to move towards uncertainty for the potential of discovery.

Bernadette Jiwa in *Hunch* (Jiwa, 2017) explains that the word curiosity comes from the Latin *cura* – to care. She identifies three forms:

1. **Diversive curiosity:** A hunger for novelty (eg social media scrolling)

2. **Empathetic curiosity:** A drive to understand another person by trying to see the world as they do

3. **Epistemic curiosity:** A focused quest to understand, ask, and connect ideas

Empathetic and epistemic curiosity are essential in creating an authentic hospitality culture. They inspire us to ask better questions, empathise deeper to form meaningful connections with ideas and people, improve systems, and drive transformation in experiences and organisational culture.

Caution: The shadow side of curiosity

Unchecked curiosity can spiral into distraction or detachment from reality. The same spark that drives discovery can cause shiny-object syndrome – an uninformed obsession with chasing fads and the latest trends. Genuine curiosity does not just chase dots; it connects them.

Be mindful of unbalanced curiosity that lacks grounding. Insight without discernment and follow-up action becomes indulgence that rots credibility, undermines team cohesion, and causes operational inefficiencies.

Watch for signs of intellectual arrogance, fear, and the need to always be right, as these can lead to a disconnection from the positive value of healthy curiosity. People who resist curiosity may fear judgement or an unsettling shake to their world and their perceived position within it.

Some people are afraid of appearing unsure or losing control. Others have been taught that curiosity is nosy, socially unwelcome, or unsafe. However, hiring someone resistant to exploring new and different avenues, or someone who is convinced they already know everything, can shut down valuable insights from other perspectives and entrench outdated thinking that blocks growth.

The business case for curiosity

You may be familiar with the saying *Curiosity killed the cat*. This serves as a cautionary tale discouraging risk taking, disruption, and disturbing the status quo. However, in today's turbulent, non-linear world, avoiding curiosity entirely represents a missed opportunity. Curiosity motivates us to explore more about the unfamiliar or the ambiguous and to chart a new course around dangers and towards fresh opportunities.

To help your hospitality business survive and thrive, you need to have curiosity crackling within your teams, encouraging them to challenge stale thinking, ask bold questions, and drive continuous improvement. Promote principled rebellion as a cultural value to help check siloed thinking and smug complacency.

Research shows that curiosity drives innovation, sharpens decision-making, enhances team performance, and improves adaptability in uncertain conditions (Gino, 2018). For hospitality brands operating in fast-paced environments, harnessing curiosity provides an undeniable competitive advantage.

A report in the *Harvard Business Review* (Kashdan et al, 2018) identifies five dimensions of curiosity:

1. **Deprivation sensitivity:** Drive to resolve gaps in knowledge
2. **Joyous exploration:** Pleasure in learning and discovery
3. **Social curiosity:** Interest in how other people think and behave, which has the strongest link with being a kind, generous, modest person.
4. **Stress tolerance:** Willingness to embrace doubt and ambiguity
5. **Thrill seeking:** A craving for new, risky experiences

Together these traits create resourceful, resilient, and responsive teams, serving as a strong antidote to blind spots and biases. When curiosity is cultivated in all areas of your operation, teams become less susceptible to confirmation bias or stereotyping (Gino, 2018).

When used positively, curiosity becomes the key that turns ordinary procedures into remarkable experiences. Here's an example: A curious front desk assistant asks returning guests, *What is one small detail that would make your stay memorable?* This simple question, acted on, sparks the creation of personalised welcoming rituals – from handwritten book quotes to never-tried-before food and hand-picked playlist links – turning standard stays into cherished moments of surprise.

Why curiosity matters – impact snapshot

Curiosity fires up the instinctive desire to explore and understand. Once activated and channelled, discoveries that can lead to change and transformation become more likely. Hire for curiosity, and you will create a culture inhabited by questioners and explorers – people who are naturally attuned to learning and finding new and better ways to create unforgettable experiences.

- **Guest experience impact:** Curiosity inspires custom-crafted experiences, and new ways to create joyful surprise and improve systems and processes.

- **Team culture impact:** Curiosity fuels empathy, creativity, learning, experimentation, and a collective growth mindset.

- **Business impact:** Curiosity is vital for creating a culture of continuous improvement, innovation, and long-term agility and protecting against stagnation.

BOLO ALERT

Signs of genuine curiosity:

- A relentless questioner, asking thoughtful, unexpected, deep questions
- Evident intuition, spontaneous ideas, and unconscious musings
- Sharing of credible examples of cross-disciplinary exploration beyond comfort zones
- Sense-making – desire to understand why and how things work, leading to fresh insights
- Consistent balance of inquiry and follow-through
- Stories of surprise, discovery, change, and growth
- Genuine fascination with new ideas, experiences, people, and places

Signs of superficial or absent curiosity:

- Superficial or performative questions, showing a reluctance to question deeply and regularly
- Difficulties in sharing credible stories of cross-disciplinary exploration and aha moments from unexpected sources
- Reluctance to move from the familiar, showing an avoidance of adapting or changing
- Resistance to considering and adopting alternative viewpoints and methods – a *That's how we've always done it* bias
- Intellectual posturing – vulnerability or courage not evident in stories shared
- A focus on fleeting fads, interest without insight, or insight without meaningful application

> **Pro interviewer tip**
>
> Look for candidates who are curious about people and places. They proactively venture down rabbit holes, exploring new ideas and disciplines, and return with valuable insights and actionable steps.

Questions to uncover curiosity

Here are just a few examples of questions for you to build on, to enable you to determine your candidate's capacity for curiosity.

 Exploring understanding

- Is curiosity good, bad, or both? Please explain your reasoning. (Interview tip: Curiosity in itself has no moral virtue.)

 Exploring curiosity in action

- On a scale of 1 to 10, with 10 being the highest, how curious are you? Please provide examples to illustrate.

 Delving deeper

- When did you last explore something completely new or out of your comfort zone?
- What sparked your curiosity?

- What did you discover?
- How did it make you feel?

❓ Understanding individual curiosity traits

Quick-fire round – complete the sentence without overthinking:

- I have always been curious about...
- I am currently intrigued by...
- I do not understand the fascination with...

❓ Discovering personal stories

- What small everyday things fascinate you?
- How do they make you feel?

16
Super Skill 4: Creativity

Creativity is not a finite resource; it multiplies the more we engage with it. A quote often attributed to celebrated poet and civil rights activist Maya Angelou captured this truth succinctly: 'You can't use up creativity. The more you use, the more you have' (Ardito, 1982).

Creativity is both a mindset and a practice fuelled by cross-pollination of ideas, remixing, and connecting the dots.

Tania Katan (2019) champions 'creative trespassing' – brave acts of imagination that sneak wild ideas into stale and predictable environments. There are no hacks; you must step outside the lines. Explore what is possible, probable, and profitable. This is how innovative cultures flourish.

The power of creativity

In *Creative Calling* (Jarvis, 2019), Chase Jarvis defines creativity as 'the practice of combining or rearranging two or more unlikely things in new and useful ways.' Creativity is the drive to question norms, observe the familiar with fresh eyes, frame problems as puzzles to be solved, and imagine alternative and better paths forward.

We now know that creativity is not the domain of lone geniuses – that myth has been debunked. Adam Grant points out that original thinkers are not necessarily the first, but they are the ones brave enough to act differently and persistently (Grant, 2016).

The opposite of creativity? Conformity. Creativity challenges norms and frees the maker mindset.

James Victore issues a bold invitation to 'feck perfuction' (Victore, 2019), a rallying cry to rebels who choose progress over polish. You will discover this kind of creativity in team members who dare to ask *Why?* and *What if...?*

To lock this in, logic and ego must step aside. As advertising icon Dave Trott writes, 'We need to let go of our prejudices and pre-formed opinions. To remove the straitjacket of conventional wisdom. Only then can we have a mind clear enough to think the unthinkable' (Trott, 2019).

In daily operations, creativity fuels solutions, improvisation, and service recovery. When plans unravel, systems stall, and guest service falters. This is when creative hospitality alchemists shine with originality, empathy, resilience, and flair.

Caution: The shadow side of creativity

Creativity without purpose alignment becomes chaotic. Untethered ideas can overwhelm teams and clog workflows. Overconfident originality, untempered by humility, dazzles but often fails to deliver. Ideas developed in isolation might seem innovative, but they often lack meaning or relevance; in reality, they are driven by ego and untested by reality.

Beware of creativity theatre: brainstorming meetings without follow-through. The outcome? Instead of ideas that get actioned, they become recurring agenda items.

The business case for creativity

In hospitality, creativity is the seasoning that transforms service into experience. Without it customised connections and experiences that bring unexpected delight would be impossible. Whether it is a concierge personalising a welcome ritual or a housekeeper's handwritten note tucked into towel origami, these acts of care and connection are signed by creativity.

Here is an example of what can happen when creativity is allowed to flow freely in teams. A commis chef becomes curious about a little-used local spice and begins experimenting with it off-shift. Inspired, the head chef organises a culinary-team tasting session, led by the commis. A novel flavour item becomes a catalyst for inspired food conversations. What follows is a new signature dish that delights guests and rekindles creativity across the brigade.

This was not a flashy initiative. The commis chef did not wait for permission from his boss – it was his quiet passion and curiosity that kicked off a new culinary adventure. This is creativity in action: curiosity paired with follow-through, trust paired with latitude, and experimentation leading to innovation. All this resulted in the creation of a new signature dish with a compelling origin story worth sharing.

Ditch the scarcity mindset and embrace limitless creativity. As Dave Trott reminds us, 'Creativity, once you have learned to spot it, is your legal unfair advantage' (Trott, 2019).

Why creativity matters – impact snapshot

By hiring for creativity, you are rewiring your organisation for adaptability, reinvention, and longevity.

- **Guest experience impact:** Creativity leads to delight, surprise, signature service, and standout experiences.

- **Team culture impact:** Creativity energises collaboration, experimentation, and collective learning and improvisation.

- **Business impact:** Creativity reinforces brand edge, relevance, and distinctiveness through creative problem solving and innovative practices.

BOLO ALERT

Signs of genuine creative brilliance:

- Willingness to boldly question norms with irreverent context-awareness
- The balance of wild imagination with real-world execution
- Delight in exploring, iterating, and sharing outcomes
- Vulnerability, curiosity, and collaboration
- Inspiration drawn from unexpected sources and disciplines
- Creative wins and failures shared as learning opportunities

Signs of surface-level creativity:

- The use of buzzwords without depth
- Propensity to follow trends without adapting them
- Tendency to default to policies without challenge

- Avoidance of feedback or constructive critique
- Untested ideas pitched with no path to action
- Inclination to tinker without skill, impact, or purpose

Pro interviewer tip

Hire creative rebels with a cause. Look for story-rich examples of rebellion with empathy, cross-disciplinary ideas, collaboration, and the courage to build alternative paths.

Questions to uncover creativity

Here are just a few examples of questions for you to build on, to enable you to determine your candidate's capacity for creativity.

 Understanding lived experience

Describe a time you approached a familiar task or routine duties in an unconventional way.

- What sparked the idea?
- What happened next? (Interview tip: Check for resistance to or acceptance of the idea.)

Gauging personal levels of creativity

- What passion or interest outside of work influences your creativity?
- Why do you do it?

SUPER SKILL 4: CREATIVITY

 Discovering personal stories

Share a time when you broke a rule to improve something.

- What was the risk?
- What was the reward?

 Delving deeper

- What hidden skill or experience sparks your creativity? (Interview tip: Invite answers off the official records, ie not included in the candidate's CV/résumé.)

 Living the spirit of collaboration

- How have you encouraged someone else's creativity?

17
Super Skill 5: Unlearn Learning

Unlearn learning is the process of letting go of outdated mindsets and practices, while simultaneously allowing your curiosity and courage to fly you to new insights.

Futurist Alvin Toffler wrote, 'The illiterate of the 21st century will not be those who cannot read and write, but those who cannot learn, unlearn, and relearn' (Toffler, 1970).

Unlearn learning is a practice of openness and mental agility, sifting, and sorting. It means consciously retaining relevant knowledge while letting go of obsolete beliefs, behaviours, or ideas – even ones we have long cherished – and embracing new ones that serve our current reality and position us to meet the future better prepared. Unlearn learning is where vulnerability meets courage and empathy dances with curiosity.

The capacity to unlearn-learn hinges on two principles (Dweck, 2007):

1. **Intellectual humility:** The courage to recognise and acknowledge when we don't know something.
2. **Psychological flexibility:** The ability to adapt our thoughts and actions when faced with uncertainty and change.

The power of unlearn leaning

In *Atlas of the Heart,* Brené Brown writes, 'People who demonstrate intellectual humility don't lack confidence or conviction [...]. Humility allows us to admit when we are wrong – we realise that getting it right is more important than needing to "prove" that we are right' (Brown, 2021).

This Super Skill is especially relevant in the hospitality industry, where change is constant and expectations are constantly shifting. Holding too tightly to 'what worked before' is a recipe for irrelevance. When you unlearn, you remain agile and stay open to new ideas and innovation. When you learn and apply the lessons, you keep your edge.

Cultural humility matters too. Its absence feeds xenophobia and narrow thinking. Anna Katharina Schaffner notes, 'Humility ... is associated with xenophilia, an attraction to foreign cultures' (Schaffner, 2020). This broadens minds and deepens understanding, which is particularly vital for authentic hospitality.

Caution: The shadow side of unlearn Learning

Unlearning without discipline turns into flakiness. Jumping from trend to trend without discernment causes confusion, not growth. A blasé approach – devoid of intellectual rigour, questioning, or analysis – can lead to superficial solutions and systems that are unable to meet the challenges of uncertainty and change.

Conversely, a stubborn attachment to old beliefs – driven by ego, fear, or the sunk-cost fallacy – hinders progress and growth for both individuals and organisations. The practice of consistent unlearning learning requires intellectual humility and a willingness to let go of old ideas. Billionaire investor and lifelong learner Charlie Munger considers this deliberate abandonment as not only wise but also essential: 'Rapid destruction of your ideas when the time is right is one of the most valuable qualities you can acquire. You must force yourself to consider arguments on the other side' (Munger, 2005).

The business case for unlearn learning

When the world shifts, sticking with yesterday's truths is a fast track to irrelevance. Holding on to past success can seem safe, but it can also be a trap. Unexamined systems turn into blind spots that lead to decline.

Picture a restaurant clinging to outdated service rituals. As the world changes, customers leave, talented employees follow, culture stagnates, and the business stalls, all because no one stopped to ask, *Is this still working?*

Now, consider this story: A luxury island resort, facing fraying team dynamics and poor guest feedback, tried something radical – monthly twenty-four-hour role swaps. HR joined landscaping. Spa worked with F&B. Housekeeping partnered with front office. The goal? To unlearn assumptions, see each other through new eyes, and build bridges between departments. This was not an HR-led cross-training or career-upskilling programme. What followed was connection, laughter, respect, and a shared sense of purpose. It shifted mindsets from siloed service delivery to a shared responsibility for the guest experience, gradually rewiring the culture. Both the guests and the team felt the difference.

Unlearn learning in action is about building a culture that thrives on empathy, curiosity, and shared learning.

Hire mental trapeze artists – individuals who readily shed outdated mindsets and practices then swing forward, soaring and bringing colleagues along with them. During uncertain times and stormy conditions, they will help your business bend, not break.

Why unlearn learning matters – impact snapshot

With unlearn learning firmly in place, Creativity has more space to expand.

- **Guest experience impact:** Unlearn learning ensures a curiosity-led service and innovative guest experiences.

- **Team culture impact:** Unlearn learning boosts a culture of learning, experimentation, adaptation, and co-creation.

- **Business impact:** Unlearn learning drives organisational agility and adaptability powered by humility and bold learning.

BOLO ALERT

Signs of genuine unlearn learning capability and practice:

- Readiness to confidently admit what they do not know
- The search for fresh, even opposing, perspectives
- Real examples shared of mindset or habit shifts

- Ability to abandon old beliefs when faced with better evidence
- Refusal to tie identity to credentials and past success
- Use of feedback and setbacks to grow
- Willingness to share new learnings to uplift others

Signs of underdeveloped unlearn learning mindset and practices:

- Defence of the old ways without good reasons
- Resistance to change and alternative perspectives, avoiding feedback
- Over-reliance on outdated success stories, titles, and credentials
- Reluctance to admit lack of knowledge or being in the wrong
- Apparent openness but lacking evidence to show development and growth

---

Pro interviewer tip

Seek candidates who balance vulnerability with courage, curiosity with empathy.

They are natural knowledge sharers, comfortable being uncomfortable as they learn and develop. They explore, adapt, and help keep the business culture nimble.

SUPER SKILL 5: UNLEARN LEARNING

Questions to uncover unlearn learning

Here are just a few examples of questions for you to build on, to enable you to determine your candidate's capacity for unlearn learning.

 Gauging unlearn learning

- How do you approach learning something completely new?
- How do you best learn?

 Understanding lived experience

- What is a practice or belief you have recently changed your mind about, and why?

Delving deeper

- When was the last time you said, 'I don't know'?
- What happened next?

Discovering personal stories

Think about three individuals who taught you something surprisingly valuable.

- What did they teach you?

Discerning the strength of humility
- When was the last time you were proved wrong or were mistaken about something?
- What happened? How did you respond? How did you feel?

18
Super Skill 6: Gratitude

Practising gratitude strengthens bonds through heartfelt recognition and appreciation, laying the foundation for a culture that encourages loyalty.

Gratitude is the practice of recognising and valuing people, the good things in our lives, and the benefits of unexpected events or changes in circumstances that initially seemed negative. It fosters a warmth that persists when someone is truly seen and appreciated, or after receiving kind thoughts and deeds.

In a community setting, it is more than simply saying thank you; gratitude actively acknowledges and celebrates the contributions of others, amplifying trust, loyalty, and a sense of belonging, and deepening human connections.

The power of gratitude

Brené Brown describes gratitude as 'an emotion that reflects our deep appreciation for what we value, what brings meaning to our lives, and what makes us feel connected to ourselves and others.' While gratitude begins as an emotion, she says, its true power emerges when it becomes a consistent practice (Brown, 2021).

Dr Robert Emmons, a leading researcher on gratitude, identifies two key components (*Greater Good Magazine*, no date):

1. Recognising goodness in our lives
2. Acknowledging that this goodness comes partly from external sources, reinforcing humility and interconnectedness

Gratitude is inherently social. It reminds us that many of life's best things such as support, generosity, and accomplishments are the result of the contribution of others, not just of our own effort. We cannot do it all alone.

Remain vigilant about the dangers of taking people and things for granted. 'Complacency shows in a lack of awareness of others and an absence of gratitude' (Blyth, 2015). Neglect and complacency towards comforts, privileges, and people gradually erode relationships and weaken connections.

Think of gratitude as your culture's natural connection fertiliser; it nourishes relationships and helps the entire system flourish.

Caution: The shadow side of gratitude

Crucially, gratitude must be sincere and unburdened by ulterior motives. Strategic or performative gratitude can diminish bonds, breed mistrust, and undermine team culture.

Gratitude loses its connective power when it feels transactional or superficial. A perfunctory thank you with no detail, 'interest' shown only out of obligation, or care that feels hollow will quickly strip the exchange of trust and meaning. A thank you without heart closes doors.

Misdirected flattery, fawning, or favour-seeking can lead to resentment, creating a perception of favouritism and division. For example, when the director of rooms singles out the efforts of front-of-house guest services for recognition while overlooking the housekeeping team's handling of a large guest checkout, it creates resentment and disunity, dampens honest feedback, and erodes the hard-won cross-departmental unity essential for seamless service.

Toxic gratitude, which involves convincing ourselves or others that there is so much to be grateful for, can be used as a tool to limit people. It can keep them small and disconnected from reaching their fullest expression of true selves or contributing more and making a greater impact.

Here are two ways toxic gratitude can be experienced:

- **Self-limiting.** Being grateful can serve as an excuse for settling or avoiding the pursuit of one's dreams or ambitions. Someone might be grateful for a job because it fulfils its utility – usually because it pays the bills – but this often comes at the expense of hiding that person's entire personality or gradually draining their spirit.
- **Oliver Twist treatment.** In Charles Dickens's novel (Dickens, 2003), when Oliver Twist asks 'Please, sir, I want some more' of the gruel for himself and the other starving occupants of the workhouse, it leads to him being harshly punished by authority figures, who are shocked and outraged. They interpreted his ask as defiance and a threat of rebellion.

Similarly, in workplaces, telling someone that they are in a fortunate position (eg because they are the first woman ever to hold the role) and should be thankful or that they are ungrateful for seeking more – such as a promotion, pay rise, or learning opportunities – can expose a system that subtly or openly punishes those who strive to excel. This reaction, which limits others for the comfort of some or to preserve the status quo, illustrates the darker side of recognition.

The business case for gratitude

Through the act of genuine and meaningful recognition and appreciation, gratitude boosts individual and collective wellbeing, enhances collaboration, and fortifies community spirit. When practised consistently by every team member, regardless of seniority, over time, gratitude actively reduces selfishness and entitlement. Otherwise, if allowed to take hold in the culture, these two corrosive traits can result in disengaged rote work as well as routinely cold service delivery from employees who have mentally checked out due to feeling unappreciated.

In human-first environments such as true hospitality, a culture infused with gratitude boosts morale and encourages generosity – a desirable quality often found in the most celebrated hosts. Gratitude plays a vital role in cultivating psychological safety. Amy Edmondson found that appreciation fosters an environment where people feel seen, heard, and valued – essential for innovation, creative risk taking, and effective service recovery (Edmondson, 2018).

Regular gratitude practices also build emotional resilience. They equip individuals to manage stress and sustain positivity, even when pressure runs high (Wood, Froh, and Geraghty, 2010).

In an article for Forbes, Eric Mosley (2019) demonstrates that gratitude leads to measurable business benefits: increased productivity, stronger employee engagement, higher retention, and greater customer satisfaction.

Why gratitude matters – impact snapshot

Gratitude is cultural oxygen – invisible yet vital. When it flows, it energises connections and makes both guests and colleagues feel recognised. Without it, service becomes robotic and culture deteriorates and wilts.

- **Guest experience impact:** Genuine gratitude makes guests feel recognised and remembered, transforming ordinary service into loyalty-building moments.

- **Team culture impact:** A culture of appreciation strengthens trust and boosts morale; colleagues who feel valued naturally extend that care to one another and to the company.

- **Business impact:** Gratitude enhances retention, engagement, and productivity; it grounds your brand in positive energy that attracts the right employees as well as guests.

BOLO ALERT

Signs of genuine gratitude:

- Prompt and sincere expression of feelings of meaningfu appreciation
- Credible stories shared of regular gratitude practice
- Clear examples of recognising others' contributions in a personalised way
- Reflective stories shared of gratitude during hardship or challenges
- Examples of sincerely giving before receiving
- Comfort in expressing and receiving gratitude
- Authentic and generous recognition of others' brilliance
- Healthy gratitude fuels growth: thankfulness forms a basis for pursuing goals and living purposefully

Warning signs of surface-level gratitude:

- Woolly responses and examples of gratitude in practice that lack credibility
- Overly polished responses lacking emotional depth and conviction
- Misalignment between the action and the appreciation described
- Gratitude recognised as a burdensome obligation rather than a valuable practice
- Gratitude seen as transactional
- Acts of gratitude lacking specificity or meaning to the receiver

- Discomfort when discussing receiving or giving thanks
- Gratitude twisted into complacency: thankfulness becomes an excuse for settling for less or not pursuing goals or purpose.

> **Pro interviewer tip**
>
> Look for candidates who naturally elevate others with personalised, meaningful expressions of appreciation that recognise valuable contribution and effort.
>
> Gratitude is a personal motivator and a generator of good karma.

Questions to uncover gratitude

Here are just a few examples of questions for you to build on, to enable you to determine your candidate's capacity for gratitude.

(?) Exploring capacity for gratitude

- What are you thankful for right now?
- What do you want to be thankful for in the future?

(?) Understanding lived experience

Describe a recent instance where you expressed appreciation.

- Who did you thank, and why?
- How did you demonstrate your gratitude?
- How was it received?
- Why was it meaningful to both the receiver and to you?

(?) Measuring the spirit of generosity

- What does the saying 'pay it forward' mean to you?
- How do you practise this philosophy?

(?) Discovering personal stories

- What has been the most meaningful act of generosity you have received?
- Was it expected or unexpected?
- How did it make you feel?

(?) Responding to the absence of gratitude

- How do you feel when your contribution or efforts go unnoticed?
- Please share a time when this happened. How did you respond?
- How does that affect how you express gratitude to others?

19
Super Skill 7: Vulnerability

Vulnerability is a catalyst for strong moral courage. It is an ultimate indicator of authentic human spirit that is hard to fake.

Vulnerability is the willingness to be seen, even when we cannot control the outcome or the reactions of others. It involves showing up with courage, honesty, and emotional openness without thoughts of winning or losing. It is a public display of inner strength, even though it is often seen as a weakness that should be kept hidden.

In many societies, concealing your true self is standard practice. After all, removing the mask and taking a break from constantly being 'on stage' allows the genuine self and a natural state of being to surface.

Choosing to appear publicly with vulnerability is an act of bravery, especially when the stakes are high. It might lead to a loss of personal comfort, peace, and even in some cases safety. It is during moments of exposure, though, that the chance for real human connection arises.

The power of vulnerability

The opportunity to glimpse the genuine person behind the public face is like receiving a handwritten personal invitation embossed with bravery and sealed with hope. Honour it with the respect it deserves.

Brené Brown defines vulnerability as the emotion we experience during times of uncertainty, risk, and emotional exposure (Brown, 2021). Her studies and research findings make it clear that there is no courage without vulnerability. In a world obsessed with perfection, control, and performance, we must show up in our full humanity, embracing our flaws and feelings with the courage to 'embrace the suck'. Running from our vulnerability is pointless, because it is an inescapable part of being a social human. Instead, Brown advises leaning into it in alignment with our values. Therefore, she says, 'Vulnerability is not weakness; it is our greatest measure of courage.'

In a McKinsey & Company article interview (McKinsey & Company, 2022), Will Guidara, Michelin-starred restaurateur and author of *Unreasonable Hospitality* (Guidara, 2022), echoes the truth that vulnerability is vital for exceptional hospitality that resonates on a high emotional frequency: 'I don't believe that two people have the capacity to connect unless they both have their guards down, and one of the best ways to get people to relax is to lead with vulnerability.'

Vulnerability creates space for self-improvement and operational correction, the grace to grow, and honest communication loops that enhance the guest experience, business operations, and internal cultural dynamics. To access this sacred space, individuals must remove their social masks and lay down the excess baggage of perfectionism, blame, and image management. What remains is clarity and an unedited human being who is more likely to form stronger, authentic connections based on who they truly are, with their flaws and fabulousness.

Caution: The shadow side of vulnerability

Vulnerability is not oversharing or a licence to offload emotions without boundaries. As Brown cautions, vulnerability without discernment can erode trust just as much as withholding (Brown, 2021).

Mock vulnerability – used to manipulate, garner pity, or evade accountability – degrades integrity and team trust. You may recognise some of these examples: emotional meltdowns, hiding mistakes, or dodging feedback; or projecting polished perfectionism, which only breeds fear and fractures teams.

Failing to embrace vulnerability with healthy responses such as humour or light-heartedness can lead to fragility and rigidity. Tension in oneself and others is increased during challenging moments that require a relaxed state to defuse the situation and move forward. On the contrary, demonstrating your vulnerability as a Super Skill means that authenticity, curiosity, courage, and emotional maturity guide your words and actions, even when your knees threaten to buckle and your stomach flips somersaults.

The business case for vulnerability

Vulnerability enables individuals and teams to build trust, communicate openly, share ideas, learn from failures, and form genuine human connections. When vulnerability is embraced as a superpower, it holds open the door for resilience to enter as a counterbalance. Both vulnerability and resilience are crucial for team members to actively engage in the practice of continual unlearning, learning, and the courage to flex their creative muscles.

When vulnerability is modelled by leaders, a psychologically safe environment is created, inspiring teams to do the same. Truth telling and transparency become a regular part of interactions and communication.

Consider the high stakes involved when a financial controller makes a calculation error in the monthly financial reports or capital-expenditure proposal. In a workplace where vulnerability is normalised, there are fewer people hiding mistakes, blaming others, or shirking responsibility. Support for openness encourages team members to be more willing to take responsibility and ownership for their actions, whether good or bad. When vulnerability is respected and supported, it creates a foundation of trust and active accountability, enabling learning among team members more effectively than any off-site management retreat.

By embracing vulnerability leaders can inspire their teams to do the same. You will be rewarded with a culture where leaders and teams are more likely to manage costly risks to people and the business, and continuous improvement and innovation become a positive benefit to the operation.

Admitting when you don't know something, asking for help, or acknowledging mistakes are not signs of failure; they are signs of strength. Hospitality teams that embrace courageous vulnerability become more adaptable, empathetic to genuine issues and opportunities, and capable of managing high-pressure guest issues and business-critical situations with swift and decisive responses. When vulnerability is paired with courage and clear boundaries, it promotes stronger connections, accountability, and caring team collaboration.

When vulnerability is valued, it helps encourage individuals expand their agency, social confidence, and self-worth. It fosters a team culture where brave openness is contagious, learning is encouraged, and trusted work environments become a reality. Vulnerability is the Super Skill that boosts the ROI of realness. It is a radiant human quality that expresses our unfiltered, authentic emotions and lays the foundation for deep connection based on our true selves, not the masks we wear.

Why vulnerability matters – impact snapshot

By hiring for vulnerability, you recruit individuals who are willing to be open, take risks, experiment, fail, get back on their feet, embrace their humanity, and inspire others to do the same.

- **Guest experience impact:** Vulnerability enhances compassion, authenticity, transparency, engagement, and emotional presence in service moments.

- **Team culture impact:** Vulnerability builds trust and care, encourages learning, and supports a psychologically safe environment for improvement and experimentation.

- **Business impact:** Valuing vulnerability enables agility, faster learning cycles, innovation, and stronger human connection.

BOLO ALERT

Signs of genuine vulnerability:

- Comfort in sharing knowledge gaps, mistakes, and what has been learned
- Expression of uncertainty or discomfort with honesty and self-awareness
- Responsibility taken for feedback or failure, with awareness shared of how it encouraged development and growth
- Warm humour to defuse tension and foster connection, including laughing at themselves
- A grounded sense of self-worth with clear, healthy boundaries

Signs of vulnerability avoidance or unhealthy use:

- Vulnerability being seen as weakness and avoided in self and others
- Setbacks glossed over, fault dodged, or blame shifted
- Signs of perfectionism, people pleasing, or hiding behind a polished façade
- Oversharing without boundaries or personal stories used to evade accountability
- Mocking of others to deflect attention; reluctance to laugh at own missteps
- Avoidance of moving from 'thinking mode' and of sharing how they truly feel

> **Pro interviewer tip**
>
> In the interview, take time to build trust and an atmosphere where your candidate feels free to share thoughts, feelings, and stories openly.

Questions to uncover vulnerability

Here are just a few examples of questions for you to build on, to enable you to determine your candidate's capacity for vulnerability.

(?) Exploring understanding

- Is vulnerability good, bad, or both? Please explain your reasoning. (Interview tip: Vulnerability in itself has no moral virtue.)
- How do you typically show vulnerability?

(?) Gauging vulnerability

- What is it that most people do not know about you that you wish they knew? (Interview prompt: A hidden skill, know-how, experience, hope, or dream?)

(?) Understanding lived experience

- Which criticism affected you the most?
- Why did it sting?
- How did you process it, and what did you learn?

Honouring vulnerability

- How can we assist you in that area? (Interview tip: This is with reference to the previous question.)

Discovering personal stories

- When did you last laugh at yourself, and what was the reason?

20
Super Skill 8: Courage

Moral courage is the steadfast commitment to act with discernment and conviction, inspiring principled, transformative outcomes.

Courage is not about conquering fear; it is about deciding to act despite fear. Genuine courage means choosing truth over approval, bold moves over conformity, discernment over rash action, and vocal values over quiet regret.

Courage is the resolute vow to navigate the world in harmony with your values, even when fear and uncertainty are present, and when resistance is inevitable. It is determined by action guided by conscience. Aristotle defined courage as principled action, despite fear, for what is right and honourable (Aristotle, 2020).

Some people shy away from discomfort. Others confront it consciously and vulnerably, with their eyes wide open and a fire in their belly. They grow into courage.

The power of courage

As poet and civil rights activist Maya Angelou powerfully states, 'Courage is the most important of all virtues because, without courage, you cannot practice any other virtue consistently' (Ju, 2008).

Courage flows through the veins of transformational characters and super-connectors. You will recognise courageous integrity when individuals:

- Act according to their values without waiting for permission or authority
- Do the right thing, even with uncertain outcomes and inevitable discomfort
- Use their voice against wrongdoing, despite personal risk
- Champion the underdog and the powerless by exposing injustice

Brené Brown (2021) gives this definition: 'Integrity is choosing courage over comfort; it's choosing what's right over what's fun, fast, or easy; and it's practicing your values, not just professing them.'

Not all courage is equal. Philosopher Susan Sontag reminds us that courage alone is not enough – moral courage is essential and the most significant (Popova, no date). Moral courage means speaking up for others and advocating dignity, respect, fairness, and natural justice. Look for signs in your candidate's stories when hiring for human magic. For example, consider the courage of their conviction to speak up, stand alone, act ethically, and lead with truth in the face of understandable fear and anxiety.

Caution: The shadow side of courage

Courage without discernment can at best fail to make a positive difference and at worst lead to unnecessary risks. False courage, driven by ego, drives people to avoid discomfort and duck out of making tough decisions and taking necessary action.

Sometimes people fail to show courage because they have legitimate fears of being attacked or condemned for their position, point of view, or what they represent. Whether the threat is real or imagined, the feeling is genuine and can lead to courage being silenced.

Blind courage or performative outrage lacking compassion results in moral tyranny rooted in self-righteousness. Genuinely brave people regularly reevaluate their actions and acknowledge their mistakes, understanding that true courage involves both bold acts and humble self-awareness.

Suppressing courage leads to stagnation, complicity, burnout, and potential decay. Resistance appears futile, and the status quo persists. As Todd Kashdan states, conforming, rationalising, and legitimising numb us to accept oppressive norms (Kashdan, 2022).

Margaret Heffernan warns that when moral courage is stifled, toxic cultures thrive as individuals fear speaking out and being vilified, ostracised, or worse (Heffernan, 2020). The remedy is to employ individuals with moral courage and protect them.

The business case for courage

In hospitality, moral courage manifests in simple yet powerful ways during daily operations. For example: the general manager who enforces the hotel's house rules by personally relocating a celebrity VIP guest, causing an unacceptable mess and damage to their suite while showing disrespect to the room attendants servicing the room; or the commis chef who dares to confront the sous chef's bullying behaviour disrupting the kitchen team's energy. These micro-acts of valour build trust, strengthen reputation, and foster psychological safety, essential for human magic to sparkle.

A McKinsey global survey (McKinsey & Company, 2021) revealed that while psychological safety is essential for team performance, only a small percentage of leaders consistently exhibit the behaviours that foster it. When leadership behaviour lacks courage, innovation, ethical decision-making, and personal accountability falter. Therefore, cultivating courage is vital for individual integrity and for assembling resilient, high-performing teams that can create extraordinary experiences.

Moral courage often resides in small acts – a quiet yet firm no, a refusal to accept the convenient wrong over the uncomfortable right, honest apologies, and hard truths shared kindly. Hire for moral courage, and you recruit a fire starter for transformation.

Why courage matters – impact snapshot

When hiring for human magic, courage is essential; it unlocks all other Super Skills and gives us the bravery to practise them consistently.

- **Guest experience impact:** Courage fuels committed, values-aligned experiences and care, especially under pressure.

- **Team culture impact:** Courage builds psychological safety, challenges toxic norms, lights hope, inspires change, and develops follow-worthy leaders.

- **Business impact:** Courage increases ethical leadership and whole team behaviour, bold innovation, and resilience under uncertainty and brand reputation.

BOLO ALERT

Signs of genuine moral courage:

- Willingness to speak up, with clarity and respect, despite unpopularity
- Disposition to walk away from misaligned roles or relationships
- Ability to tap into vulnerability as a superpower – admitting mistakes and learning from them
- Tendency to champion underdogs, the underserved, and oppressed groups
- Demonstration of ethical discernment
- Ability to question norms, challenging the status quo by exploring alternative and innovative ways
- Stories shared that show moral courage and strength
- Willingness to inspire and support others to act courageously

Signs of courage avoidance or empty bravado:

- Avoidance of challenges and change to protect comfort or status, also dissuading others from challenging and questioning the status quo
- Stories and examples of moral courageous action that lack conviction and credibility
- Conflation of aggression with courage
- Fears or vulnerability hidden or dismissed
- Reluctance to admit mistakes
- Resistance to unlearning, learning, and relearning

- Propensity to quickly conform, accept groupthink, and avoid discomfort
- High tolerance for misaligned roles or unethical behaviour

> **Pro interviewer tip**
>
> You are looking to hire individuals whose principled stance transforms interactions, protects and defines moments into heroic deeds, and inspires others too.

Questions to uncover courage

Here are just a few examples of questions for you to build on, to enable you to determine your candidate's capacity for courage.

(?) Exploring understanding

- How do you define courage?
- What does it feel like to you?
- What happens when courage is absent?

(?) Understanding lived experience

Tell me about the bravest decision you have made.

- Why was it brave?
- What was the impact?

- What did you learn?
- Would you do it again?

❓ Delving deeper

Describe a situation when you chose to stay silent but later wished you had spoken up.

- What was the cost of your silence?

❓ Gauging capacity for courage

Imagine living courageously for a month. Describe what that would be like.

- What would you do?
- What is holding you back?

❓ Discovering personal stories

- How have you supported someone's act of moral courage.
- What happened?
- How did they respond?
- How did you feel?

21
Super Skill 9: Resilience

Resilience does not mean standing soldier-tall in the storm. Instead, it is about learning to bend rather than break.

Resilience is the ability to adapt, navigate complex feelings in the face of life's inevitable setbacks and uncertainties, and grow from the experience. It includes mindsets and practices that develop emotional flexibility

Susan David (2016) explains that this ability to *bounce* differentiates emotionally agile individuals in handling setbacks as they know how to adapt; align their actions with their values; and make incremental, powerful changes that lead to a lifetime of growth.

Resilience is more than bouncing back; it is the ability to regroup, adapt, and bounce forward stronger.

Emotional agility involves holding setbacks lightly, facing them bravely and compassionately, and then moving past them with hope rooted in action and realistic optimism that things will improve.

Numbing emotions or stubbornly grinding through pain does not prove resilience. As Adam Grant points out in his X post, 'Resilience isn't about immunity to pain. It's about finding the strength to withstand strain' (Grant, 2021). He goes on to explain that hardships gradually start to feel less burdensome, and instead of trying to overcome them all immediately, it's fine to live with them until they are easier to resolve.

The power of resilience

Todd Kashdan's research on psychological flexibility (Kashdan, 2022) reveals that resilient individuals efficiently label and manage their emotions, which enables them to direct their energy towards meaningful pursuits. Furthermore, resilience draws on the power of community and human connection. Its strength stems from supportive alliances rather than solo heroics.

Understanding resilience within a specific context is crucial. In some situations, resilience involves showing up when every instinct urges you to withdraw. Here presence signifies strength and hope for a better outcome. In other cases, resilience requires a strategic distance that brings clarity to and a sharper focus on essential information to guide suitable plans and actions.

Awareness and discernment guide the most prudent response to resilience. We cannot always control what happens to us, but we can choose how we respond.

Caution: The shadow side of resilience

Resilience gets a standing ovation, but what is actually happening behind the scenes?

Persisting in soldiering is not always wise, as pushing through without pausing risks burnout, bitterness, and emotional exhaustion. When we tough it out so hard, we become brittle on the inside and ultimately more likely to break. Unchecked, this stoicism morphs into resentment and detachment. What begins as strength becomes self-silencing, and human qualities such as a sense of fairness, empathy, kindness, compassion, and courage get distorted in the name of mental toughness

Forced cheer, false positivity, or shrinking yourself to keep the peace may seem like a coping mechanism. In fact, they are a betrayal of self, undermining authenticity and corroding the bonds that sustain human-centred workplaces.

Here is a deeper risk: over-reliance on resilience can mask dysfunction. In the workplace, high-performing individuals and teams may mask toxic leadership, unrealistic demands, or poor systems, all under the guise of being resilient. Running on an operation fuelled by the team's willpower is unsustainable. As the Resilience Institute cautions, resilience without reflection may lead people to absorb more stress than they should, normalising pressure and eroding the very wellbeing resilience is supposed to protect (Resilience Institute, 2023).

More than inner toughness, healthy resilience depends on relationships, psychological safety, and flexible systems – not heroic endurance alone. Too much emphasis on individual bounce-back can unintentionally normalise overwork, discourage vulnerability, and stigmatise support-seeking (Resilience Institute, 2023).

This begs the question: Can you still call it resilience if it costs you what makes you you?

A grit-only mindset is outdated and lacks the benefit of allowing grace and space to reassess. It ignores the nuance, context, and emotional self-awareness that make resilience a positive Super Skill, not a dangerous liability.

Still tempted to white-knuckle your way through? True resilience does not mean constant endurance or emotional suppression. As Jay Unwin reminds us, 'Real resilience isn't just about endurance. It's about recognising when to pull back and recover so you don't burn out completely' (Unwin, 2025).

We need to understand when to grip the wheel, and when to pull over for a rest and reflect on the prudent way forward.

The business case for resilience

Think back to March 2020, when the World Health Organization declared COVID-19 a pandemic. The global upheaval that followed was brutal but also revealing. It led to the following questions:

- Why did some businesses survive and bounce forward, while others broke apart?
- What made some teams thrive and evolve in the chaos, while others floundered?

In his book *Antifragile*, Nassim Nicholas Taleb (2012) offers an answer: systems that thrive under stress aren't just resilient; they are *antifragile*. Fragile things break under pressure, and resilient things withstand it. Antifragile systems are strengthened by volatility, not weakened by it, because they use stress, disruption, and uncertainty as fuel for growth.

This is not just a philosophical idea. It is also a practical lens in Human Magic Hiring. Businesses often focus on system resilience with protocols such as data backups, disaster preparedness, and response plans. In reality, systems are only as adaptable and responsive as the people who operate them. The ability of your business to bend without breaking depends on your people.

Hiring for bounce-forwards beats bouncing back

What do you gain when you hire for resilience to unlock your team's collective Super Skill – adapting, recovering, caring for each other, and improving under pressure? The answer is a team that is adept at faster recovery and able to rally more strongly, particularly when efforts and mindsets are anchored to shared values, common purpose, and a sense of real-world optimism.

It's important you assemble a team of connectors who possess true resilience as well as emotional intelligence and self-awareness, so that they know when to pause, regroup, respond, and reinvent.

In my years working in locations that are paradisaical but vulnerable to hurricanes, I have seen how extraordinary teams not only survive the chaos that follows terrible devastation; they turn that chaos into a creative possibility, embody the best of humanity, make meaning from it, and serve with grace, all with a side of courage and humour.

Resilience embodies an indomitable spirit, characterised by quiet strength that allows bending without breaking, adaptation without sacrificing core values, and uncovering hidden potentials. When you assemble a team primed for resilience, you embrace the enduring energy that enables people and cultures to adapt and grow stronger through adversity and seize unexpected opportunities.

Why resilience matters – impact snapshot

Hire for proven resilience, and you not only strengthen your team but also take steps to future-proof your business.

- **Guest experience impact:** Resilience creates considered, responsive service and emotionally intelligent experiences, especially in the face of operational challenges and chaos.

- **Team culture impact:** Resilience boosts trust, creative thinking, learning forward, mutual support, collective flexibility, flow, and growth.

- **Business impact:** Resilience strengthens the business from the inside by enhancing cultural and operational adaptability, which increases the chance of surviving and thriving in uncertain and rapidly changing landscapes.

BOLO ALERT

Signs of genuine emotional resilience:

- A balanced outlook – hopeful yet grounded in reality
- A range of emotional and physical tools to navigate stress
- Strong support systems and nurturing networks
- Ability to remain calm under pressure and respond with self-control
- Adaptability and flexibility in the face of change or setbacks
- Ability to learn and unlearn with humility and reflection
- Grace and compassion offered to themselves and others
- Understanding of when to ask for help and willingness to receive it
- A clear moral compass – actions aligned with values

Signs of fragile or underdeveloped resilience:

- Superficial positivity masking denial or inaction
- Avoidance, numbing, or emotional disconnection in storytelling
- Hero complex – over-reliance on grit without reflection or support
- Rigid thinking and behaviour patterns, being resistant to feedback
- Reluctance to delegate, trust, or seek help when needed
- Lack of support systems and nurturing networks

- F at or minimal empathy for others' experiences
- Values that feel vague, performative, or unanchored in action

> **Pro interviewer tip**
>
> Look for individuals who are self-aware of their emotional needs and empathise with others. They share credible stories about how they have bounced back and forward, becoming stronger, better, and wiser through the experience.

Questions to uncover resilience

Here are just a few examples of questions for you to build on, to enable you to determine your candidate's capacity for resilience.

 Revealing inner strength

- What helps you get back on your feet when life knocks you down?

 Exploring understanding

- How do you determine when to quit, persevere, or pivot?
- What signals do you look for to guide your action?
- Please share a specific story about when you either stuck it out, quit, or pivoted.

Gauging ability to bounce back and bounce forwards

- What practices do you have in place to support your emotional and physical wellbeing?

 Understanding lived experience

My grandmother used to say, 'Nothing good comes easy'.

- What accomplishment are you most proud of, and why?
- What obstacles did you overcome to achieve it?

 Delving deeper

- Reflecting on your last significant challenge, what unexpected skills or strengths did you discover?

22
Super Skill 10: Purpose Connection

Purpose-connected teams intensify your brand's impact. When personal purpose and organisational purpose align, human magic is powered up exponentially.

Purpose connection involves aligning personal principles, talents, and aspirations with meaningful work and contribution. It serves as a guiding North Star, helping individuals navigate challenges and build resilience. Additionally, it acts as a beacon that encourages embracing opportunities and staying motivated by creating impact.

The power of purpose connection

Viktor Frankl (1946) summarised it best: 'Those who have a "why" to live can bear almost any "how".' Having survived a Nazi concentration camp, Frankl demonstrated through his own experience and real-life observations that his idea of logotherapy – the belief that personal meaning is vital for resilience and personal growth – is accurate. The concept applies equally to personal and professional contexts.

Simon Sinek (2010) echoes this in *Start with Why*, reminding leaders that sustainable long-term performance is driven not only by technical skills but also by a deep connection to the purpose behind the work, specifically to who and what their efforts serve.

A common misconception is that purpose is static. In truth, it evolves, but when someone connects to their *why* and infuses meaning and clarity into their everyday work, transformative magic happens.

Beware of lofty mission statements or mantras telling you to follow your passion. They can trap you in a dreaming loop, with no decisive action taken to turn the vision into reality. Purpose-connected action is defined by tangible alignment with the work and authentic *who* of an individual or organisation. Individuals with a strong sense of purpose tend

SUPER SKILL 10: PURPOSE CONNECTION

to bring presence, pride, and clarity to their roles. In hospitality, where human connection is the product, purpose connection is a non-negotiable strategic pillar that operational action plans and team goals must support.

Caution: The shadow side of purpose connection

When poorly understood, purpose connection can backfire. Vague or woolly purpose language can confuse, as the loss of clarity leads to disconnection and an aimless drift off course. Meanwhile, false purpose – when someone inherits or copies goals or values that are not truly theirs – can lead to disillusionment.

Over-identifying with work can become risky when roles change or end, or when recognition fades. If purpose is tied too tightly to external outcomes, people flounder when they shift roles or lose status. Romanticised ideas about purpose or finding your calling, without committed action, can cause frustration and disillusionment when reality does not match dreams. Purpose-driven egos can also damage team culture. Real purpose connection means contribution to the collective cause, not just personal fulfilment.

The healthiest form of purpose connection is flexible and values-led, with clear, actionable steps and accountability built in.

HELP WANTED

The business case for purpose connection

Purpose-connected people stay longer, contribute more fully, create deeper emotional connections with guests and teammates, and turn employees into proud brand advocates. They strengthen the trust fabric of your culture, creating a culture of 'ownership', unity, and collective resilience.

The outcome? A business culture where people show up not only to do tasks but also to make meaning every day creates an unmistakable difference that is felt by guests and the team. Just like yeast in a perfect loaf, purpose lifts performance from within.

In hospitality, where human-created experiences are the product, this emotional commitment creates a sustainable edge and an uncopyable advantage over industry peers.

> 'We connect to each other around our beliefs. Our beliefs also help us to connect more deeply with ourselves. Our beliefs drive behaviour... Successful businesses are built on being believed and believed in, not just noticed.'
> —Bernadette Jiwa (2014)

A white paper (Antonio-Gadsdon and Tingsager, 2022) affirms that successful leaders link company purpose to individual belief and motivation, providing people with systems and stories that enable them to see their role as valuable, unique contributors to the entire organisation.

Why purpose connection matters – impact snapshot

Purpose-aligned, energised teams serve with sincerity, act with ownership, and deliver your brand promise with conviction.

- **Guest experience impact:** Purpose-led teams serve with authentic conviction, empathy, and intentionality.

- **Team culture impact:** Purpose connection strengthens unity, resilience, shared ownership, and accountability across teams.

- **Business impact:** Purpose connection unites team hearts and minds behind a common, clear purpose that acts as a behaviour guide and reminder in stable and uncertain times. It increases engagement, retention, and values-based leadership at every level. It also strengthens culture and brand reputation for the long haul.

BOLO ALERT

Signs of genuine purpose connection:

- Clear sense of fulfilment and personal drive
- Stated aspirations and purpose ring true to their character and values
- Motivation from making a difference, not just making money
- Stories of impact, meaning, and value-based action
- Alignment between past decisions and personal values
- Curiosity about how their work contributes beyond themselves
- Consistent commitment toward a personal aspiration or vision

Signs of misaligned or absent purpose:

- Generic, clichéd responses about passion, calling, or success
- Lack of conviction about their stated *why*. Check – does it belong to your candidate, or is it a borrowed purpose or an inherited calling?
- Over-focus on titles, accolades, or personal brand
- Little self-awareness about values or impact
- Misalignment between stated beliefs and actions
- Little interest in shared purpose or collective outcomes

> **Pro interviewer tip**
>
> Purpose-connected people light up when they talk about how they contribute to making meaning, creating a difference, or adding value. Their stories reflect impact, not ego.
>
> Hire those who care deeply and consistently act with conviction.

Questions to uncover purpose connection

Here are just a few examples of questions for you to build on, to enable you to determine your candidate's capacity for purpose connection.

 Exploring understanding

- What is a goal or cause that gives your work deeper meaning?
- What are you doing to move toward it?
- What is holding you back? (Interview tip: Probe behaviour, mindset, or resource obstacles.)

 Gauging purpose connection in action

- On a scale of 1 to 10, how aligned are your daily actions with your values? (Interview tip: Ask for examples.)
- What is something you have said 'no' to recently, and why?

(?) Delving deeper

- What is the 'price' you refuse to pay for success?

(?) Understanding aspirations

- What change in the world do you want to be part of?

(?) Uncovering purpose-related ambitions

- How do you want to be remembered?
- What would you like your obituary to say?

Conclusion: If Not Now, When?

Having read this book to the end, you now understand the difference between believing in human magic and taking action to achieve Human Magic Hiring.

You have a choice. Do you take the brave path or the business-as-usual road?

The usual road appears safer. It is crowded with what everyone else is doing – job posting, the usual person spec, a standard competency checklist, and a well-worn interview script.

However, you and your business are not like everyone else's. You know that traditional interviewing alone no longer works, and certainly not for the kind of human-led, hospitality-driven business you are creating. That is why you are here, reading this book.

You are not looking for more culture *fit*. You want culture *lift*. Your business does not only need more headcount. It needs individuals who show up purposefully every day and raise the bar simply by being fully present in the room. That means assembling an entire team with a knack for creating moreish, meaningful, memorable moments.

Here is the challenge: Human connection cannot be commanded. It must be earned, given freely, and nurtured with trust. That means hiring hospitality alchemists – your ensemble of rebels with empathy, free thinkers with flair, creators of experiences, and connectors with courage. That kind of human magic does not appear in traditional interview scripts or conventional competency-based questions.

Thinking about bolting this new framework to a conventional, competency-based hiring process? That is like grafting new rootstock onto a dead tree – no fruit will grow. There is no hack or shortcut, but there is a clear path. You must reimagine, redesign, and commit to prioritising humans over resources, capital, or assets.

You say you want magic, but will you redesign your system to allow it in or continue to toe the line?

The truth is that the block is never about a complete lack of Super Skills or the seemingly elusive magic.

The block is the mindset and the culture. You must remove the obstacles from the door and invite magic in. That's because human magic responds to a genuinely honest invitation – one that sounds like, *Let us build something real and meaningful. Something that matters, just like you do.*

The moment is now

Yes, the world is messy and chaotic. Tech is faster. AI is smarter. Budgets are tighter. So much all around us feels shaky and sapped, creating cultures of regurgitated sameness. In an era of networking and hyper-connection, we are becoming increasingly disconnected from what makes us human.

Human-to-human connection is the rarest, most treasured prize remaining. Reclaim it and restore it to its rightful place in the heart of your operation as the crown jewel of your unique business advantage.

Do not let the promise of shortcuts, scale, and speed seduce you away from your craft. Use technology for transactions and convenience, but keep deep, nuanced, and multilayered connections in human hands. Let your team's combined Super Skills, personal agency, and authentic human presence transform hospitality into art and alchemy. The brighter future belongs to those who co-create hospitality and build businesses with it together.

Here is the good news: You do not need permission or 'perfect conditions'. You need only laser-focused intention and the will to start today.

Improving the hiring process and enhancing the candidate experience are essential parts of the process. Deciding what you want your brand to be known for is the crucial preliminary step you would be unwise to skip.

What will you build?

Building a profitable business with excellent service is vital, but that is just the beginning. You are shaping a hospitality brand that stands out from the crowd. One that people talk about with joyful admiration and respect, and that they love, want to defend, and feel a sense of connection and belonging to. To achieve this, you need an extraordinary team, united behind your company's vision and values.

Are you brave enough to do what it takes? The recruitment rules that once made sense now seem arbitrary, outdated, and meaningless. Worse still, they may hinder your business growth.

The hospitality alchemists you need are already waiting for you. They will not appear by chance. They will be revealed when you break with hiring orthodoxies and conduct interviews in a different way.

CONCLUSION: IF NOT NOW, WHEN?

Your guests, your team, and your community will notice your difference and become captivated, beating a path to your door. That is because hospitality served with purpose and people at its heart becomes magnetic, irresistible, and magical.

Here is your crossroads moment. The real question is not whether Human Magic Hiring will work. The question is whether you will do it now that you know how, because if not now, when?

Use this guide to break free from the constraints of traditional interview practices and gain an edge over competitors by assembling your own extraordinary team of hospitality alchemists. Keep it close. Mark it up. Make it yours. Just please do not alter the framework or supporting system, as doing that may weaken the potency of the Human Magic Hiring impact.

Knowledge without action is a missed opportunity, and time is not your ally. Start slowly and trust the process. As the saying goes, the proof of the pudding is in the eating. The risk is not in trying something new. The real danger is staying the same and believing it will keep you safe.

HR needs more rule breakers. Hospitality needs more alchemists. Lead onwards by assembling your team to build your business, with this book as your hiring guide. To make that possible, start with bold, consistent Super Skills interviewing that will shape your culture.

Next steps

Feel free to spread the word about this book. Share what you learn about Human Magic Hiring, and let us build the movement. If you do that, my mission (for now) will be complete.

If *Help Wanted* has sparked ideas or improved your hiring experience, I'd love to hear about it. You can contact me via my website at www.bananapepperhr.com to share how this guide is helping you summon and sustain human magic in your organisation.

Want to take it further? What do you have in mind – using it for commercial work or training, remixing the material, or incorporating it into a larger project? Brilliant, but please ask me first.

For commercial use or larger integrations such as using the Three-Course Conversation interview framework, the ten Super Skills question bank, and the BOLO system in a paid workshop, deck, or toolkit, or republishing excerpts exceeding 100 words, you will need to obtain explicit written permission first. Get in touch. Who knows where that great new connection might lead?

Now it is over to you. Rewrite the rules. Write the new story of hospitality. The rest? That is up to you to create as your own legacy.

Bibliography

Antonio-Gadsdon, N and Tingsager, M (2022) 'The six tenets of agile hospitality: Six tenets every leader needs to survive and thrive in the new era of hospitality', Bizimply, https://images.g2crowd.com/uploads/attachment/file/1248968/The-Six-Tenets-Of-Agile-Hospitality-FINAL.pdf, accessed 14 August 2025

Ardito, M (1982) 'Creativity: It's the thought that counts', *Bell Telephone Magazine*, 62(1), American Telephone and Telegraph Company

Arefin, D (2024) 'How to pollinate vanilla orchids', *The Garden Fixes*, https://thegardenfixes.com/how-to-pollinate-vanilla-orchids, accessed 15 August 2025

Aristotle (2020) *One Swallow Does Not Make a Summer*, Penguin Classics

Ayyappan, S (2025) 'Forget AI sentience: Authenticity should be our focus in marketing', *MarketingProfs*, www.marketingprofs.com/articles/2025/52619/authenticity-vs-generative-ai-in-marketing, accessed 9 August 2025

Barnes, V (2021) *Free Happiness: The art and science of positivity*, self-published

Batson, CD and Shaw, LL (1991) 'Evidence for altruism: Toward a pluralism of prosocial motives', *Psychological Inquiry*, 2(2), 107–122, https://doi.org/10.1207/s15327965pli0202_1

Bennett, N and Lemoine, GJ (2014) 'What VUCA really means for you', *Harvard Business Review*, https://hbr.org/2014/01/what-vuca-really-means-for-you, accessed 15 August 2025

Blyth, L (2015) *The Little Pocket Book of Kindness: How to love life, laugh more and live longer*, CICO Books

Boutique Hotelier (2023a) 'Robin Hutson', *Boutique Hotelier*, www.boutiquehotelier.com/hotelier-profiles/robin-hutson-who-is-he, accessed 9 August 2025

Boutique Hotelier (2023b) 'It's important we double down on the founding principles of what a Pig is about', *Boutique Hotelier*, www.boutiquehotelier.com/the-pig-hotels-ceo-on-expansion, accessed 9 August 2025

Britell, A (2022) 'Caribbean Hotelier: Gregor Nassief of Secret Bay in Dominica on luxury', *Caribbean Journal*, www.caribjournal.com/2022/08/21/caribbean-hotelier-dominica-secret-bay, accessed 19 September 2025

Brown, B (2021) *Atlas of the Heart: Mapping meaningful connection and the language of human experience*, Random House

Calderone, A (2023) 'How to get a reservation at The Lost Kitchen, one of the hardest-to-book restaurants in America', *People*, https://people.com/food/how-to-get-a-reservation-at-the-lost-kitchen-maine-erin-french-postcards, accessed 15 August 2025

Chang, D (2019) *Eat a Peach: A memoir*, Clarkson Potter Publishers

CIPD (2024) 'Benchmarking employee turnover: What are the latest trends and insights?', CIPD, www.cipd.org/uk/views-and-insights/thought-leadership/cipd-voice/benchmarking-employee-turnover, accessed 8 August 2025

Clark, B (2023) 'How to use the "Rule of Three" to create engaging content', Copyblogger, https://copyblogger.com/rule-of-three, accessed 11 August 2025

David, S (2016) *Emotional Agility: Get unstuck, embrace change, and thrive in work and Life*, Avery Publishing Group

Dickens, C (2003) *Oliver Twist*, Penguin Classics

Dweck, CS (2007) *Mindset: The new psychology of success*, Random House

Dweck, M and Kershaw, G (Directors) (2020) *The Truffle Hunters*, Sony Pictures Classics

Edmondson, AC (2018) *The Fearless Organization: Creating psychological safety in the workplace for learning, innovation, and growth*, Wiley

eHotelier (2023) *The Industry's Future Skills Needs – Why skills are so important to the future of the industry*, eHotelier, https://ehotelier.com/research/hotel-skills-whitepaper, accessed 8 August 2025

Farnam Street (2021) 'Episode 115: Danny Meyer: Hospitality and humanity', *The Knowledge Project Podcast*, https://fs.blog/knowledge-project-podcast/danny-meyer, accessed 9 August 2025

Farnam Street (no date, a) 'Avoid organizational empty suits at all costs', *FS blog*, https://fs.blog/empty-suits, accessed 11 August 2025

Farnam Street (no date, b) 'The power of questions', *FS blog*, https://fs.blog/power-questions, accessed 11 August 2025

Frankl, VE (1946) *Man's Search for Meaning*, Beacon Press

Gallup (2025) *State of the Global Workplace: Understanding employees, informing leaders,*

Gallup, www.gallup.com/workplace/349484/state-of-the-global-workplace.aspx, accessed 8 August 2025

Gartner (2025) *Talent Strategy for Growth: A CHRO's guide,* Gartner, www.gartner.com/en/human-resources/insights/reinvent-your-talent-strategy, accessed 8 August 2025

Gilbert, E (2015) *Big Magic: Creative living beyond fear,* Riverhead Books

Gino, F (2018) 'The business case for curiosity', *Harvard Business Review,* https://hbr.org/2018/09/the-business-case-for-curiosity, accessed 13 August 2025

Godin, S (2010) *Linchpin: Are you indispensable?,* Penguin Group

Godin, S (2014) 'Two magical sentences missing from most job ads', *Seth's Blog,* https://seths.blog/2014/02/two-magical-sentences-missing-from-most-job-ads, accessed 9 August 2025

Godin, S (2018) 'We can do better than meeting spec', *Seth's Blog,* https://seths.blog/2018/04/we-can-do-better-than-meeting-spec, accessed 19 September 2025

Godin, S (2020) 'Meeting spec (doing the minimum)', *Seth's Blog,* https://seths.blog/2020/05/meeting-spec-doing-the-minimum, accessed 19 September 2025

Grant, A (2013) *Give and Take: Why helping others drives our success*, Viking

Grant, A (2016) *Originals: How non-conformists move the world*, Viking

Grant, A (2021) 'Resilience isn't about immunity to pain. It's about finding the strength to withstand strain. You don't need to overcome all [...]', X, https://x.com/AdamMGrant/status/1456246020954804232, accessed 22 May 2025

Greater Good Magazine (no date), 'What is gratitude?', https://greatergood.berkeley.edu/topic/gratitude/definition, accessed 19 September 2025

Guidara, W (2022) *Unreasonable Hospitality: The remarkable power of giving people more than they expect*, Portfolio

Hackman, S (no date) 'Beethoven X. Beyoncé', Steve Hackman, www.stevehackman.com/beethoven-x-beyonce, accessed 15 August 2025

Hammond, C (2023) *The Keys to Kindness: How to be kinder to yourself, others and the world*, Canongate Books

Heffernan, M (2020) *Wilful Blindness: Why we ignore the obvious at our peril*, Simon & Schuster

Hemingway, E (1926) *The Sun Also Rises*, Charles Scribner's Sons

Jarvis, C (2019) *Creative Calling: Establish a daily practice, infuse your world with meaning, and succeed in work + life*, HarperCollins

Jiwa, B (2014) *Difference: The one-page method for reimagining your business and reinventing your marketing* [ebook], The Storytelling Press

Jiwa, B (2015) *Meaningful: The story of ideas that fly*, Perceptive Press

Jiwa, B (2017) *Hunch: Turn your everyday insights into the next big thing*, Portfolio

Jiwa, B (2018) *Story Driven: You don't need to compete when you know who you are*, Perceptive Press

Ju, A (2008) 'Courage is the most important virtue, says writer and civil rights activist Maya Angelou at Convocation', *Cornell Chronicle*, https://news.cornell.edu/stories/2008/05/courage-most-important-virtue-maya-angelou-tells-seniors, accessed 15 August 2025

Kashdan, T et al (2018) 'The five dimensions of curiosity – How are you curious?', *Harvard Business Review*, https://hbr.org/2018/09/the-five-dimensions-of-curiosity, accessed 13 August 2025

Kashdan, T3 (2022) *The Art of Insubordination: How to dissent and defy effectively*, Penguin Random House

Katan, T (2019) *Creative Trespassing: How to put the spark and joy back into your work and life*, Crown Currency

Kleon, A (2012) *Steal Like an Artist: 10 things nobody told you about being creative*, Workman

Mastroianni, A (2022) 'Good conversations have lots of doorknobs', *Experimental History*, www.experimental-history.com/p/good-conversations-have-lots-of-doorknobs, accessed 11 August 2025

McKinsey & Company (2021) 'Psychological safety and the critical role of leadership development', McKinsey & Company, www.mckinsey.com/capabilities/people-and-organizational-performance/our-insights/psychological-safety-and-the-critical-role-of-leadership-development, accessed 14 August 2025

McKinsey & Company (2022) 'Author talks: Hospitality lessons from a Michelin-star restaurateur', McKinsey & Company, www.mckinsey.com/featured-insights/mckinsey-on-books/author-talks-hospitality-lessons-from-a-michelin-star-restaurateur, accessed March 2025

Merriam-Webster (no date) 'A lesson on "unmoral", "immoral", "nonmoral", and "amoral"', Merriam-Webster, www.merriam-webster.com/grammar/using-unmoral-immoral-nonmoral-amoral, accessed 15 August 2025

Meyer, D (2006) *Setting the Table: The transforming power of hospitality in business*, HarperCollins

Mikkelsen, K and Martin, R (2016) *The Neo-Generalist: Where you go is who you are*, LID Publishing

Morelli, SA, Lieberman, MD, and Zaki, J (2015) 'The emerging study of positive empathy', *Social and Personality Psychology Compass*, 9(2), 57–68, https://doi.org/10.1111/spc3.12157

Morgan, J (1996) *Debrett's New Guide to Etiquette and Modern Manners: The indispensable handbook*, Headline Publishing

Mosley, E (2019) 'The business impact of gratitude', *Forbes*, www.forbes.com/sites/ericmosley/2019/11/27/the-business-impact-of-gratitude, accessed 22 October 2025

Munger, C (2005) *Poor Charlie's Almanack: The wit and wisdom of Charles T Munger*, Donning Company Publishers

Popova, M (no date) 'Susan Sontag on moral courage and the power of principled resistance to injustice', *The Marginalian*, www.themarginalian.org/2012/12/05/susan-sontag-on-courage-and-resistance, accessed 15 August 2025

Rao, S (2016) *Unmistakable*, EP Dutton & Co Inc

Resilience Institute (2023) 'Are there downsides to resilience?', Resilience Institute, https://resiliencei.com/blog/are-there-downsides-to-resilience, accessed 25 June 2025

Roya, W (2019) 'Golden rules for magic that every beginner should know', PCD, https://playingcarddecks.com/blogs/all-in/golden-rules-for-magic-that-every-beginner-should-know, accessed 11 August 2025

Schaffner, AK (2020) 'What is humility and why is it important? (Incl. Examples)', *PositivePsychology.com* blog, https://positivepsychology.com/humility, accessed 13 August 2025

Schwandt, TA (2015) *The SAGE Dictionary of Qualitative Inquiry*, SAGE Publications

Scott, K (2017) *Radical Candor: Be a kick-ass boss without losing your humanity*, St Martin's Press

Segnit, N (2010) *The Flavour Thesaurus: Pairings, recipes and ideas for the creative cook*, Bloomsbury Publishing

Sinek, S (2010) *Start with Why: How great leaders inspire everyone to take action*, Portfolio

Spencer, V (2025) 'Mirepoix is the foundation of stews, sauces, and more—here's how to make it', Martha Stewart, www.marthastewart.com/268585/mirepoix, accessed 10 August 2025

Sutherland, R (2019) *Alchemy: The dark art and curious science of creating magic in brands, business, and life*, William Morrow

Taleb, NN (2012) *Antifragile: Things that gain from disorder*, Random House

BIBLIOGRAPHY

Taylor, S (2005) *People Resourcing*, Chartered Institute of Personnel and Development

Toffler, A (1970) *Future Shock*, Random House

Trott, D (2019) *Creative Blindness (And How to Cure It)*, Harriman House

Tsui, S (no date) 'Bey-thoven (Sam Tsui × Carnegie Hall Ensemble Connect) Unofficial Mashup', https://youtu.be/5csLgmrhWvQ, accessed 11 August 2025

Umami Information Center (no date), 'Umami basics', www.umamiinfo.com/what/whatisumami, accessed 19 September 2025

Unwin, J (2025) 'Resilience isn't just pushing through... It's knowing when to rest', Functional Resilience, https://jayunwin.substack.com/p/resilience-isnt-just-pushing-through, accessed 14 August 2025

Victore, J (2019) *Feck Perfuction: Dangerous ideas on the business of life*, Chronicle Books

Wood AM, Froh JJ, and Geraghty AW (2010) 'Gratitude and well-Being: A review and theoretical integration', *Clinical Psychology Review*, 30(7), 890–905, https://doi.org/10.1016/j.cpr.2010.03.005

Zingerman's (no date), 'Bios of founders and managing partners', Zingerman's Community of Businesses, www.zingermanscommunity.com/press/bios-of-founders-and-managing-partners, accessed 9 August 2025

Further Resources

Blyth, C (2009) *The Art of Conversation: A guided tour of a neglected pleasure*, Gotham Books, published by Penguin Group

Brown, B (2010) 'The power of vulnerability', TEDGlobal, www.ted.com/talks/brene_brown_the_power_of_vulnerability, accessed 15 May 2025

Brown, B (2018) *Dare to Lead: Brave work. Tough conversations. Whole hearts.*, Random House

Campbell, J (1949) *The Hero with a Thousand Faces*, Princeton University Press

Chin, C (no date) 'Copying better: How to acquire the tacit knowledge of experts', *Commoncog*, https://commoncog.com/how-to-learn-tacit-knowledge, accessed 15 August 2025

Chin, C (no date) 'The three kinds of tacit knowledge', *Commoncog*, https://commoncog.com/three-kinds-of-tacit-knowledge, accessed 15 August 2025

Chiseri-Strater, E and Sunstein, BS (1997) *Fieldworking: Reading and writing research*, Blair Press

David, S (2017) 'The gift and power of emotional courage', TEDWomen, www.ted.com/talks/susan_david_the_gift_and_power_of_emotional_courage, accessed 23 May 2025

Emmons, R (2010) 'Why gratitude is good', *Greater Good Magazine*, https://greatergood.berkeley.edu/article/item/why_gratitude_is_good, accessed 13 August 2025

Farnam Street (no date) 'Carol Dweck: A summary of growth and fixed mindsets', *FS blog*, https://fs.blog/carol-dweck-mindset, accessed 13 August 2025

Farnam Street (no date) 'The mental models of human nature and judgment', in: 'Mental Models: The Best Way to Make Intelligent Decisions (~100 Models Explained)', *FS blog*, https://fs.blog/mental-models, accessed 15 August 2025

Farnworth, D (no date) 'The amazingly simple anatomy of a meaningful marketing story [infographic]', Copyblogger, https://copyblogger.com/meaningful-marketing-story, accessed 15 August 2025

FURTHER RESOURCES

Godin, S (2018) 'Missing from your job description', *Seth's Blog*, https://seths.blog/2018/04/missing-from-your-job-description, accessed 15 August 2025

Godin, S (2021) 'Write a better spec', *Seth's Blog*, https://seths.blog/2021/12/write-a-better-spec, accessed 15 August 2025

Google Arts & Culture (no date) 'The Beyoncé and Beethoven mash-up you didn't know you needed', Google Arts & Culture, https://artsandculture.google.com/story/dgUx6Ge_a-n4LA, accessed 15 August 2025

Heffernan, M (2012) 'Dare to disagree', TEDGlobal, www.ted.com/talks/margaret_heffernan_dare_to_disagree, accessed 14 August 2025

Housel, M (2025) 'A few questions', Collaborative Fund, https://collabfund.com/blog/a-few-questions-1, accessed 15 August 2025

Klein, G (2016) 'Mindsets: What they are and why they matter', *Psychology Today*, www.psychologytoday.com/us/blog/seeing-what-others-dont/201605/mindsets, accessed 15 August 2025

Mandloi, R (2020) 'How to be the "purple squirrel" employers are looking for', *Harvard Business Review*, https://hbr.org/2020/02/how-to-be-the-purple-squirrel-employers-are-looking-for, accessed 15 August 2025

Marone, L (2021) 'Resilience: The power to overcome, adjust, and persevere', *Psychology Today*, www.psychologytoday.com/gb/blog/gaining-and-sustaining/202106/resilience-the-power-overcome-adjust-and-persevere, accessed 22 May 2025

Pressfield, S (2012) *The War of Art: Break through the blocks and win your inner creative battles*, Black Irish Entertainment LLC.

PsychCentral (no date) 'What resilience is and isn't', *PsychCentral*, https://psychcentral.com/lib/what-is-resilience, accessed 22 May 2025

Sinek, S (2009) 'How great leaders inspire action', TEDxPugetSound, www.ted.com/talks/simon_sinek_how_great_leaders_inspire_action, accessed 15 August 2025

Taylor, J (1973) 'Jobsworth', http://youtu.be/watch?v=fz44_Sp0K8A, accessed 15 August 2025

The HR Digest (2020) 'What are purple squirrels and unicorns?', *The HR Digest*, www.thehrdigest.com/what-are-purple-squirrels-and-unicorns, accessed 15 August 2025

Tomkins, S (no date) 'A helpful mindset: The art of befriending stress', Zeal!, www.zealcoaching.co.nz/a-helpful-mindset-the-art-of-befriending-stress, accessed 15 August 2025

FURTHER RESOURCES

Toppman, L (2024) 'A Dance of Life with Beethoven and Beyoncé', WDAV blog, https://blogs.wdav.org/2024/11/a-dance-of-life-with-beethoven-and-beyonce, accessed 15 August 2025

Utah Historical Society (2023) 'How to write field notes', Utah Historical Society, https://history.utah.gov/repository-item/how-to-write-field-notes, accessed 15 August 2025

Glossary

This brief glossary gives you helpful information for this guide to decoding human magic and hospitality alchemy.

Alchemy by numbers: The practical maths behind the art of creating meaningful and memorable human connections. Ten Super Skills can generate 120 unique guest experiences per alchemist, totalling 30,000 experiences from a team of 250 people. It makes a compelling argument for the data-driven sceptic.

ALT-HR: A bold, inventive alternative to conventional HR practices, integrating marketing principles with a focus on creativity and conscious rebellion against the status quo. ALT-HR reverses the traditional order by emphasising alignment rather than assimilation, standing out instead of blending in, storytelling instead of scorecards, hospitality over hierarchy, and business strategy led by humans rather than resources.

Brainpokes: New insights that stem from exploring diverse disciplines and cross-pollinating ideas, provocations, or questions that challenge the status quo and stimulate fresh thinking. They work to stretch the mental muscles, prick the conscience, and serve as a call to action.

Hospitality alchemist: An indispensable team member who wields their personality, practical genius, discipline, and unique human magic to create unforgettable experiences. They are never regular employees; they are your improvisers, memory-makers, culture shapers, and everyday revolutionaries, capable of transforming your operation from blah to cooking with gas, and your business from standard to stellar. Note: they do their best work when part of a jazz ensemble-style team, not as solo acts.

Hospitality alchemy: The transformative blend of Super Skills, technical expertise, and lived wisdom that turns standard service into an unforgettable human connection. It extends beyond completing essential tasks and meeting expected performance standards. When activated, it creates a soulful and sensory moment with a powerful, regenerative ripple effect that touches everyone who experiences it, like a ball of magic being passed between the creator and the receiver.

Human magic: A candidate's distinctive blend of personality, values, purpose, and tacit knowledge. Human magic is revealed through credible real-life stories, Super Skills, adversity, triumphs, joy, and values in action.

Human Magic Hiring: The first act of hospitality, incorporating the Three-Course Conversation interview framework, which transforms service into stories and teams into an ensemble of hospitality alchemists. This prioritises the candidate as hero, Super Skills interviewing, life stories, human connection, and hospitality. Designed like a nourishing meal and soul-enriching dining experience: appetiser (warm-up), entrée (deep dive), and dessert (lasting impression).

Inner life compass: Your candidate's internal GPS, which shows their exact position via the signals sent through their beliefs, values, mindset, and purpose. It fuels their unique qualities, emerges especially under pressure during critical decisions, and influences how they present themselves, navigate life, and move through the world.

ROI of realness: The tangible return on investing in human qualities of authenticity, agency, and autonomy. The ROI of Realness compounds and delivers a measurable return over time. What is the reward? Resilience, reputation, and results that you can feel.

Rule of three: The magic number for compelling interviews, interactions, and storytelling. It makes things memorable, balanced, and emotionally resonant and is used throughout this book as a framework to help structure questions and identify patterns and the hiring process design.

Super Skills: Ten deeply human, non-trainable qualities at the core of extraordinary service and meaningful experiences. They are empathy, kindness, curiosity, creativity, unlearn learning, gratitude, vulnerability, courage, resilience, and purpose connection, all naturally sourced from lived experience.

Acknowledgements

Books may have one name on the cover, but the content owes a debt of gratitude to many. Human magic is never a solo act.

Thank you for buying *Help Wanted* and for reading it – whether you are a page-by-page explorer, a chapter connoisseur, or a purposeful ideas dipper. I hope it becomes a trusted companion as you build a business simmering with soul and a standout brand, with the help of your own ensemble of extraordinary hospitality alchemists.

Every page of this guide was stirred, seasoned, and sharpened by thinkers, doers, misfits, mentors, mavericks, and magic-makers. All those people inspired, challenged, or stood beside me – from idea spark to words on the page through to a published book. This guide would not exist without the generosity of those who taught, nudged, questioned, and cheered me on as *Help Wanted* took shape.

I was fortunate to draw from a rich pantry of ideas to create this reimagined hiring recipe for the hospitality industry. As a lifelong practitioner of what Austin Kleon calls *good theft*, I see myself as more Robin Hood than Blackbeard: steal, remix, give back. As Kleon states, 'Nothing is completely original. All artists' work builds on what came before. Every new idea is just a remix or mashup of two previous ideas' (Kleon, 2012).

To the clients, collaborators, employers, and teams who shaped my thinking – thank you for the trust, the trenches, and the triumphs. Your stories and wisdom pulse through every paragraph.

To the hospitality alchemists – you floor me. Watching you work your magic every day, I see proof that when technical brilliance and natural human skills combine, there is little that can beat a business powered by its people.

To the writers, founders, researchers, discipline experts, and podcasters – you are my invisible collaborators. I stand tall on your shoulders. Your daring ideas fired up my courage to keep challenging stale hiring practices, reimagine, and write the guide I wish I had as a rookie recruiter. Thank you.

ACKNOWLEDGEMENTS

Bringing this book into the world showed me that every book needs doulas. *Help Wanted* owes its birth to the expertise, generosity, and irreverent genius of those who stood beside and cheered me on through each stage: idea, research, rough notes, procrastination, manuscript writing, draft after draft after draft.

Special thanks go to a mathematics PhD candidate, who generously helped demystify the probability concepts underpinning the framework for calculating hospitality alchemy.

Here's a roll call of inspirational beta readers whose care, feedback, and insight shaped this book. Your nudges, and the occasional shove, kept this book writing dream moving. Thank you:

- Brenda Lee Browne, Just Write – www.linkedin.com/in/brenda-lee-browne-ma-4014a044
- Dr Vikki Barnes, Positive Wellbeing – www.drvikkibarnes.com
- Jeffrey van Dyk, The Courageous Messenger – https://thecourageousmessenger.com/about-jeffrey
- Lisa Redfern, The Barefoot Trainer – www.barefoottrainerbvi.com
- Melissa O'Hara, O'Hara Solutions Group – www.oharasolutionsgroup.com

- Michael Tingsager, The Hospitality Mavericks Podcast – www.hospitalitymavericks.com
- Patrice Gordon, Eminere – www.eminere.co.uk
- Simona Barbieri, HubDot – https://hubdot.com

I deeply appreciate the support and guidance of the Rethink Press publishing team in bringing this book to life. The journey has been both rewarding and memorable.

To Chris and Lily. You remind me every day why creating workplaces full of welcome and wonder matters more than ever.

Finally, thanks to me, for a promise made and a promise kept to write the book – I did, in the end.

The Author

Nicole Antonio-Gadsdon brings jazz-inspired improvisation to HR and a knack for questioning *Why?* to find better ways. As an HR innovator, she designs workplaces and human-led strategies that counter cookie-cutter brand experiences.

Born in Antigua, raised in the UK, and rooted in Caribbean culture, Nicole has spent over twenty years challenging outdated HR practices and transforming how hospitality businesses recruit and lead extraordinary, purpose-connected teams.

She founded Banana Pepper HR, a consultancy known for its ALT-HR, marketing-integrated approach. Nicole works with luxury hotels and hospitality innovators to translate the company's distinctive brand and guest experience into compelling employer branding and people strategies, as a foundation for culture design and operational systems alignment.

As an openings veteran, Nicole has led the people and culture teams in eleven luxury hotels, private islands, and boutique resorts in the Caribbean, including Carlisle Bay, Viceroy Anguilla, and Jumby Bay. She transforms a company's vision and mission into custom-designed cultural strategies that attract, retain, and develop cohesive brand-aligned teams.

Her work involves restructuring and launching hospitality ventures. When Sir Richard Branson's Necker and Moskito Islands needed an HR upgrade to reopen after Hurricane Irma and in response to COVID-19, Nicole, as an executive team member, revised people strategies, designed systems, implemented protocols, and guided teams through these transitions.

Nicole's ALT-HR insights have been featured on podcasts such as *No BS Agency* with Pia Silva and *Hospitality Mavericks*, as well as in white papers that challenge conventional HR practices and the status quo in the hospitality industry. In 2015 she launched her creative lab, *The HR Rabbit Hole* blog, where she set out to answer the question: What if hiring were

THE AUTHOR

treated as an act of hospitality? She also searched for the missing vital secret ingredient in assembling extraordinary teams.

While exploring, the realisation hit: human magic is neither absent nor elusive. Broken hiring systems cannot summon it, and straitjacketed cultures smother it.

Fast-forward to October 2021, when Nicole began writing and gave this evolving practice a name, which ultimately became the title of this book: *Help Wanted*.

Nicole is a member of the Chartered Institute of Personnel and Development (MCIPD) and the Institute of Hospitality (MIH). She created the Three-Course Conversation interview framework, the ten Super Skills interview questions, and the BOLO system, all of which are featured in this book.

⊕ www.bananapepperhr.com

◻ www.facebook.com/bananapepperhr/about

◻ www.linkedin.com/in/nicoleantoniogadsdon

◎ @nicole.bananapepperhr